"Then **Pinkel** Said to **Smith...**"

The Best Missouri Tigers Stories Ever Told

Steve Richardson

TRIUMPH
B O O K S

Library of Congress Cataloging-in-Publication Data

Richardson, Steve
Then Pinkel said to Smith—: the best Missouri Tigers stories ever told / Steve Richardson.
    p. cm.
  ISBN-13: 978-1-57243-998-6
  ISBN-10: 1-57243-998-X
1. University of Missouri—Football—History. 2. Missouri Tigers (Football team)—History. I. Title II. Title: Best Missouri Tigers stories ever told
  GV958.U5294R52 2008
  796.332'630977829—dc22

                                        2008013492

This book is available in quantity at special discounts for your group or organization. For further information, contact:

Triumph Books
542 South Dearborn Street
Suite 750
Chicago, Illinois 60605
(312) 939-3330
Fax (312) 663-3557

Printed in U.S.A.
ISBN: 978-1-57243-998-6
Design by Patricia Frey

For my late parents, Howard and Alberta Richardson, who provided me an education at the University of Missouri and allowed me to pursue a career in journalism.

table of
contents

acknowledgments

I saw my first Missouri football game in person in 1969 when the Tigers beat Illinois in St. Louis. That year coincides with the Tigers' last Orange Bowl season and was near the end of the Dan Devine era.

Two years later, I was a freshman journalism major at Missouri and watched Coach Al Onofrio's first Missouri team go 1–10. In 1972, as a student reporter for *The Maneater*, I covered the Missouri–Notre Dame game in South Bend, a 30–26 Tigers victory after a humiliating 62–0 loss to Nebraska the previous week. Talk about a wild ride!

After two more years of watching the up-and-down Tigers, I graduated. But the era of Missouri upsets continued for several years under Onofrio and then Warren Powers in 1978. After several solid years under Powers, Missouri football slipped into the abyss of college football from the mid-1980s until the mid-1990s. Larry Smith put together back-to-back bowls in 1997 and 1998. And finally Missouri, under Gary Pinkel, has established itself as a bowl team year after year.

For more than 20 years (1976–1996) I worked for *The Kansas City Star* and *The Dallas Morning News*. Many thanks over the years to such people as Al Onofrio, Woody Widenhofer, Warren Powers, John Kadlec, and Clay Cooper who were usually very helpful in the coverage of Missouri teams. From 1979 to 1986, I was assigned regularly to Missouri football games for *The Kansas City Star*. There were a host of players during that time I conducted interviews with, including Phil Bradley and Jeff Gaylord, who offered great insight into the program. Over the years, Larry Smith and then Gary Pinkel have also been generous with their time in media settings.

In rounding up even more information for this project, thanks to the following people for personal interviews:

Joe Castiglione, Mark Jones, Dale Smith, Bill Cocos, Tom Stephenson, Bob Stull, Lynn Dickey, Todd Dodge, Dennis Poppe,

Dean Blevins, Jim Dickey, Darrell Dickey, Dave Hart, Jack Lengyel, Dick Tamburo, Steve Hatchell, Mickey Holmes, Wayne Duke, Mike Price, Carl Reese, Merv Johnson, Jim Leavitt, Gene McArtor, Tom Amstutz, John Burns, Russ Sloan, Phil Snowden, Sam Adams, Van Robinson, Martin Sauer, T.J. Leon, Duke Revard, Keith Morrissey, Hank Burnine, Joe Buerkle, and Bill Cubit.

With the renaissance of Missouri football under Gary Pinkel and quarterbacks Brad Smith and Chase Daniel, it is a time for most Tigers to enjoy some of the recent accomplishments, but they also can pause and reflect on the past. This is an effort to bring back some of those memories of Missouri football.

—Steve Richardson
Dallas, 2007

chapter 1
Don Faurot

"[Don Faurot] was one of the special people who brought Missouri into the modern age of football…. And his honesty and integrity nobody ever questioned."

—Missouri baseball coach
Gene McArtor

Moving Missouri into Football's Big-Time

College Football Hall of Fame player Don Faurot embodied the image any school would like one of its legends to portray. Ethical and honest, innovative and fiscally responsible, the former MU athlete, coach, and administrator was a loyal, true son of the state of Missouri. Faurot devoted the better part of eight decades to the Tiger athletic programs from the 1920s until his death in 1995.

With his artful scheduling of big-time opponents on the road in the late 1930s, 1940s, and into the 1950s, he laid the financial solvency for Missouri's athletic program. He devised the Split-T formation, which eventually spread to the football giants of his era. He developed a recruiting pattern of getting Missouri's top high school players to stay home. Faurot's word was gospel in Missouri, where he laid the foundation for a golden era under Coach Dan Devine from 1958 to 1970.

"I came to appreciate him more after I played," said Merv Johnson, who played for Faurot during his final season of 1956. "I felt like he had a brilliant offensive mind. His interests lay on the offensive side the ball. His assistants did more on defense. Fifteen to 20 years after I got out of college football I could see his insight in the offensive schemes that were popular after he hung it up.

"He was a guy basically who never painted any glowing pictures," Johnson continued. "He wouldn't lead a prospective coach down a primrose path. He was a guy you would like and trust to no end. He had a tight grip on finances, even as coach. His pregame meal speech was 'Don't eat the 50¢ baked potato, eat the $3.00 steak!'"

When Faurot coached in the 1930s, 1940s, and 1950s, it was a simpler time when handshake deals were more common than contracts. Faurot, however, was a keen businessman who kept Missouri's athletic books balanced and, in the process, brought big-time college football to Columbia. He kept pushing for upgrades and for seating at Memorial Stadium to be increased to more than 50,000 seats, which was finally realized after his 19-year tour of duty as MU head football coach ended in 1956.

Don Faurot served as Missouri's coach for 19 seasons starting in 1935, and also was the school's athletic director from 1935–1942 and 1946–1966. He was inducted into the College Football Hall of Fame in 1961.

"Don was an old-fashioned guy," said Wayne Duke, former Big Eight and Big Ten commissioner. "He wrote his schedules on the back of an envelope. He did business on the back of an envelope. And I don't say that to be derogatory."

One of four Faurot football-playing brothers who grew up on a farm near Mountain Grove, Missouri, in the south central portion of the state, Don was a three-sport letterman (football, baseball, and basketball). He was part of a developing legacy of MU football players competing in other varsity sports. Faurot's brothers—Fred, Jay, and Robert—later lettered for the Tigers in football in the 1930s.

Don Faurot, a light fullback, lettered for the Tigers in 1923 and 1924. He was a starter on Missouri's first postseason team in 1924, which defeated powerhouse University of Chicago, 3–0, during the regular season. The Tigers then lost to Southern California, 20–7, in Los Angeles in a postseason game arranged when the Trojans didn't get a Rose Bowl bid.

And even then, Faurot was molding his offensive coaching philosophy.

"A lot of people think the shotgun is a new weapon," Faurot revealed in 1982. "Gwinn Henry used the shotgun at Missouri when I played for him in 1923. He split the ends out about 15 yards and the backs out about 7–10. The fullback was in a spot where he could run up the middle if he wanted to and the passer was back about eight yards.

"We threw from that. So really, the shotgun is an old weapon. But we called it the spread formation. We also ran from it. We had a good passer and in those days they (opposing teams) didn't know any better than to rush six men. So we'd dump it out there behind [them]. They didn't know how to play it."

After his playing days, Faurot distinguished himself as both a coach and athletic director, and he never had to leave his native state to do so. First at Northeast Missouri State Teachers College (later Northeast Missouri State College, Northeast Missouri State University, and now Truman State University), Faurot fashioned a 63–13–3 record and also used that "spread offense," the forerunner of the shotgun.

Included in those wins by Faurot's Kirksville team was a thrashing of his alma mater, Missouri, 26–6, during the 1933 season, when Missouri was suffering through the disastrous Frank Carideo era from 1932 to 1934. Carideo, who had a 2–23–2 record at Missouri, had been a quarterback at Notre Dame under Knute Rockne from 1928 to 1930. In those days it was fashionable for schools to hire from Rockne's coaching or playing tree in trying to emulate his success.

But some of the apples fell a long way from the branches.

Similarly, in 1934, Texas hired Jack Chevigny, a former Rockne assistant and Notre Dame player. He produced only a 13–14–2 record over three seasons for the Longhorns before being fired. Carideo would have the same fate after three years. In 1934, Missouri was shut out six times and scored just 25 points in a 0–8–1 season before Carideo was axed.

Mizzou went after one of its favorite sons as coach—Faurot—even though Tiger officials couldn't pay him much.

"Being a Missouri boy, they recruited him," said Harold Burnine, a Mizzou All-America end in the 1950s. "The Missouri president invited Faurot over. They were chatting. The Missouri president said, 'You know, whatever you do, Coach, don't discuss what you are making with other faculty members. You are making a little more than the rest of them.' Faurot replied, 'I am as ashamed of the contract (because it was so low) as you are. You don't have to worry about that.'"

Not only was Missouri suffering on the field, it was suffering at the gate as well and from financial stress in the athletic department. Football needed to start paying the bills. And Faurot would have a plan for football to do so.

"He was one of the special people who brought Missouri into the modern age of football," said longtime MU baseball coach Gene McArtor, who later was an athletic administrator under several Tiger athletic directors. "He improved the financial side of it. And he played a lot of people on the road for money guarantees. And his honesty and integrity nobody ever questioned."

Paul Christman: Faurot's Jump-Start Recruit

Faurot's breakthrough season at Missouri was his fifth one, in 1939, when the Tigers won their first Big Six (the predecessor of the Big Eight Conference) championship. Faurot had gotten lucky on a Missouri recruit named Paul Christman, a St. Louis–area quarterback. Nicknamed "Pitchin' Paul," Christman was an outstanding passer who would lead the Tigers to the 1939 Big Six title and a berth in the Orange Bowl.

"Purdue said he (Christman) was too little," remembers Martin Sauer, a Missouri player, later in the 1940s. "But he put Missouri on the map."

Sauer said Missouri wound up not only with Christman, who transferred from Purdue, but two of his main targets at Maplewood High School in St. Louis, the Orf twins, Bud and Bob. Missouri already had quality players at the fullback (Bill Cunningham) and

Quarterback Paul Christman was short for his position and weighed only 194 pounds, but he was a talented runner, passer, and punter and helped put Missouri football on the map in the late 1930s.

offensive tackle positions. Offensively, Faurot finally had the tools to win a league championship, although his nonconference schedule became rather unorthodox.

"When Faurot came down from Kirksville, his theory was to play some big-money games to get gate receipts," Sauer recalled. "He scheduled teams like Ohio State. That was the financial end of it. And by playing tough teams, his theory was even though you lost to them, you learned by playing them. You got in the Big Six, then you would be playing lesser teams. Now, they just play patsies (in nonconference games) to go to a bowl. I agree with Faurot—it toughened us up back then."

Missouri played at Big Ten powerhouse Ohio State's Horseshoe, one of the country's largest stadiums, an unfathomable nine times between 1939 and 1949. The Tigers lost eight of the nine games and tied the other, but the gate receipts helped pay for stadium expansions back in Columbia and eventually put the athletic program in the black.

Missouri later went to Big Ten power Minnesota three straight times from 1943 to 1945. And Faurot's Tigers faced New York University and Fordham on the East Coast. He also scheduled series with Michigan State, Wisconsin, Texas, Maryland, Michigan, and Southern Methodist for some big paydays during the 1940s and 1950s.

From 1939 to 1941, Missouri played the vast majority of its nonconference games on the road, but still won two league championships. It didn't matter where Christman played in 1939—home or the road. He had a swagger and usually wanted to call his own number on running plays near the goal line.

Missouri was 8–1 during the 1939 regular season, with only a 19–0 loss at Ohio State, and finished with a No. 6 ranking. The Tigers fell to Georgia Tech, 21–7, in their first Orange Bowl appearance and initial bowl appearance of any kind since Faurot was a player in 1924.

"I remember seeing Christman and the Orf boys in the Orange Bowl when I was just a junior in high school when my dad took me to the game," said Van Robinson, a Missouri end in 1943 and 1944. "Christman was a stocky guy. He was not very fast. But he was a triple threat. He passed, punted, and he ran the ball. He was a tremendous athlete. That was the only time I saw him play except on film. They were beaten by Georgia Tech's speed. They were not very big, but very, very fast."

Christman made such an impression on the 1939 Georgia Tech team members that when he died of a heart attack more than 30 years later, in 1970, they sent the University of Missouri a memorial.

A New Option Offense

After Christman left Missouri following the 1940 season, Faurot, in the spring of 1941, split the T-formation, which had been introduced in 1940 by the NFL Champion Chicago Bears and former

Stanford coach Clark Shaughnessy. The T-formation placed a quarterback behind the center, in a crouched position, instead of the ball being snapped back to a quarterback or halfback five yards behind the line of scrimmage.

The new T-formation allowed for more passing to flankers and wide receivers downfield. And even on nonpassing plays, the pass receivers served as decoys to open up the running game. But that offense alone probably wouldn't suit Faurot's future quarterbacks, who wouldn't be talented passers like Christman.

Drawing upon his earlier playing days captaining the Missouri basketball Tigers, Faurot brought the two-on-one basketball fast-break concept to football with the "Split T."

He had four basic plays: the fullback dive, the quarterback keeper, the option pitch (when the quarterback attracted defenders to the ball before flipping it to an open runner on the option), and the halfback running pass. The offense would keep defenders guessing, but would always have a two-on-one blocking edge on the end, whether running inside or outside. This offense was the forerunner of the wishbone and veer option offenses, which were popularized in the late 1960s and early 1970s.

In the "Split T," Faurot also split his line, hence the name, and position. The blockers were three or four feet apart instead of closer together. This allowed for Missouri's sometimes-lesser talent in the line not to have to dominate as much in one-on-one blocking schemes and have better blocking angles on the option plays.

In 1941, Missouri led the nation in rushing with 307.7 yards a game and had the top three individual rushers (Bob Steuber, Maurice Wade, and Harry Ice) in the Big Six Conference. Ice still owns the record for Missouri average rush per carry (minimum five carries) of 30 yards (8 rushes for 240 yards) in a 45–6 victory at Kansas in 1941.

Faurot's Tigers won two straight league titles in 1941 and 1942 as the Split T offense baffled league opponents. But with World War II at hand, Faurot was called into the navy and had to leave Missouri for three seasons (from 1943 to 1945). He was replaced by Chauncey Simpson, a Faurot assistant.

In 1941, Missouri led the nation in rushing, thanks to a talented trio of runners: Bob Steuber, Maurice Wade, and Harry Ice. Steuber, shown in his 1943 college all-star uniform, was later called to help the war effort as a U.S. Naval Aviation Cadet.

During the war, Faurot coached football at Iowa Navy Pre-Flight and also at the Jacksonville, Florida, naval station, where he took the Split T concept and shared it with others.

"I do think the coaching fraternity nationally was a lot closer then than what it is now," remarked Gene McArtor. "A lot of people knew each other at the time, and when they were in the service together they shared information. I think Don was more than willing to share his ideas on the Split T."

Two of those with whom he shared his Split T information were a couple of his service coaches, line coach Jim Tatum and offensive backfield coach Bud Wilkinson. Tatum later became head coach at Oklahoma in 1946 and took Wilkinson with him. When Tatum left following the 1946 season to take the Maryland head coaching job, Wilkinson became the Oklahoma head coach.

Those two later would use the Split T philosophy and beat Faurot.

Ironically, Faurot and Missouri beat Iowa Navy Pre-Flight 7–0 in the final game of the 1942 season before Faurot left for the service. Then the well-stocked Iowa Navy Pre-Flight team beat Missouri twice, 21–6 in 1943, and 51–7 in 1944.

"He [Faurot] kind of took it easy on us one of those years," remembers Van Robinson, an end who played at Missouri in 1943 and 1944. "His team could have scored on every play. I remember in one of those games, there was this guy from Boston College, some Polish guy. He was a back who ran around all over the field. Not anybody ever got close to tackling him. He got 20 or 30 yards every carry. There was bunch of kids and 4–Fs playing for Missouri."

Missouri During World War II

Van Robinson, a native of Kansas City, Missouri, was only 16 when he enrolled at Missouri in 1943. He was attractive to Tiger coaches because he had played high school football in Clearwater, Florida, but wanted to return to Missouri and enter the world-famous School of Journalism.

"I [was] overwhelmed when I got there, no question about it," Robinson said. "I played a little bit. I got injured my first year in the first game. I was a squad man, but not enough to letter in 1943. But I hung around. In those days, there were 700 men at the university. It was at the height of the war. It was no bigger than a lot of high schools are now. They had trouble getting players. I was no great shakes as a high school player. I played end, a 165-pound end. I would not be big enough to be a water boy now."

In 1943, Missouri football games against Colorado and Fordham were canceled because of gas rationing. The Tigers compiled a 3–5 record and were bulldozed in the big-money road games at Minnesota and Ohio State.

In 1944, Missouri was 3–5–2 and played games against Arkansas in St. Louis, Missouri, at old Sportsman's Park—where the St. Louis baseball Cardinals played—and against Kansas in Kansas City, Missouri, at Ruppert Stadium, which the minor league Kansas City Blues called home. Missouri moved the games off campus to increase the attendance, which was hovering at only 6,000 or 7,000 for games in Columbia because of gas rationing.

In the 1944 season finale, the Tigers shut out Kansas, 28–0, when the Tigers unleashed 275–pound sophomore tackle Jim Kekeris as a running back against the Jayhawks before a crowd of nearly 20,000.

Robinson remembers the Tigers' secret weapon, also the Tigers' kicker, was simply too big for the Jayhawks to contain. Kekeris, who was too big to go into the service, nevertheless had good speed for a man his size.

"It was kind of fun," Robinson recalls of that game. "They didn't level off the pitching mound. I intercepted a pass and cut for the middle of the field, running up the pitcher's mound where I got tackled. I went to the sideline, and I told my coach, 'I felt like I was running uphill,' and Coach Herb Bunker said, 'Robinson, I feel like you have been running uphill all season.'"

Missouri wasn't favored in many games in those days, but the one game in 1944 the Tigers were sure they could win was at lowly Nebraska.

"Nebraska was terrible," Robinson recalls. "Chauncey said, 'These kids are hungry. We have a much better team than they do.' But he told us if we gave them opportunity early in game, they would take advantage of it. Our quarterback fumbled. Nebraska recovered on like the 5 and they scored on the first play and they went on to win, 24–20. I dropped two passes in that game right in my hand. And that was my specialty—catching passes."

Robinson's career highlight might have come in a 21–21 tie against Oklahoma in Norman that season. But it has taken about six decades and several phone calls to set the record straight.

"They were ahead, 21–7," Robinson said. "The stadium was open at both ends. And the wind was howling from the north. They were beating our brains out. Then they threw a little flat pass. I played both ways. I intercepted it and ran it back 60 yards. The OU quarterback tackled me at about the 25-yard line. He jumped on my back when he tackled me, flipped over me, and came down and injured his leg. He was out the rest of the game. We went on and scored against the wind. And we had the wind in the fourth quarter. We tied it 21–21."

But Robinson's hometown newspaper didn't do his name justice.

"In the paper the next day—and my name is Van—the headline in *The Kansas City Star* read, 'Stan Robinson interception sets up touchdown and Missouri goes on to tie OU.' It was my greatest accomplishment and they misspelled my name. Then, in 1969, I was at a game and I was looking at the program. They had a section that was called 'What Happened 10 Years Ago or What Happened 25 Years Ago.' And they had an excerpt of the 1944 Oklahoma game, 'Stan Robinson's interception sets up touchdown.' Twenty-five years later, and it's a journalism school, and they still didn't get it right. They ran a correction and they called me Van Morrison."

About five years ago, Missouri finally got Van Robinson's name right with his game-changing interception.

The 1946 Cotton Bowl Pregame

Chauncey Simpson's last year as head coach—1945—was his finest. The Tigers won the Big Six with a 5–0 record and faced Texas and Bobby Layne in the Cotton Bowl on New Year's Day in Dallas. It was Missouri's second trip to Dallas that season after beating SMU, 10–7, in early October, on big Jim Kekeris's 17-yard field goal.

Before the October 6 game, Missouri's players hardly had time to get to the game at SMU's Ownby Stadium. It was Faurot's custom that the Tigers traveled by rail and slept on the train to save money on hotels. However, the team was often cutting it close traveling to road games. This time, the Tigers arrived just four hours before the game was to kick off.

But before the January 1 game against Texas, there was a lot more leisure time. And some of the players from both teams got together.

"A bunch of these Missouri guys had been on these All-Star squads," recalled Rooster Andrews, the University of Texas team manager. "And they were all good friends of mine. They were good guys. That was the night before the Cotton Bowl. And we went over to where they were staying. We enjoyed some beverages. We stayed up pretty late because I knew Bobby could stand it. It was Bobby's way of thinking, 'Let's entertain them royally. Let's see how late we can keep them up.'

"I'll tell you who thought he was tougher than Layne was—Jim Kekeris," Andrews continued. "He kept needling Bobby that night. After about three or four beers, he said, 'I'll show you tomorrow.' Bobby said, 'Okay, Jim, we will see you tomorrow.'"

The next day, Layne had a hand in all of Texas's points in a 40–27 Longhorns victory, which stood as the highest-scoring Cotton Bowl game for 33 years, until Notre Dame's 35–34 victory over Houston on January 1, 1979.

Missouri quarterback Leon Brown, 5'8", 139 pounds, rushed 18 times for 121 yards and teammate Robert Hopkins added 125 yards on 16 carries. Missouri's 408 yards rushing is still a Cotton Bowl record more than 60 years later. The diminutive Brown was described as "the toughest piece of rawhide seen on this field in all of the Cotton Bowl Classics played to date."

After the War with Faurot

Faurot returned for the 1946 season and faced Texas in Austin his first game back, falling by a score of 42–0. But Missouri would rebound for a 5–4–1 season. The Missouri program was now stocked with older war veterans, so many that Missouri had to have a separate schedule for them, a "B Schedule."

Missouri's Nick Carras wrestles himself free of Kansas's Bud French during the Tigers' 21–7 win in Columbia in November 1948.

"They played other towns or cities, these were guys who were on the squad—not on the first two teams, maybe the third team," said Martin Sauer, who played quarterback and defensive back at Missouri from 1947 to 1949. "I went back in 1946 and went over to Rothwell Gym and I saw all the GI veterans going out for football. I didn't even think I would make team. I didn't play in 1946. I went out for spring ball in 1947 and then played.

"When I went there, Missouri was just emerging into the big time," Sauer added. "Christman broke the ice. The war came and nothing changed. Then [in] 1946 it started to emerge. I was there when it went from a mediocre, small-medium-sized university into the big time during 1947, '48, '49."

The highlight of a 6–4 1947 season was probably the 28–7 victory at powerhouse Duke, coached by Wallace Wade. The Tigers had a top-flight option quarterback in Harold "Bus" Entsminger, who had lettered in 1942, gone off to war, and returned for the 1946-48 seasons.

"Their coach knew Entsminger was very adept at running the pitch in the Split T," Sauer recalled. "Entsminger would go down the line and pitch off the end. Duke never went after the ends—they went after Entsminger. They could never catch the guy with the ball. They kept going after Entsminger, their ends crashing. And the halfback [Missouri's] was coming around the ends and made huge gains on them all day."

The postwar years also ushered in one of Mizzou's biggest fans. Bill Cocos of Lemay, Missouri, played the trumpet in the Missouri band at home football games as student in the late 1940s. Cocos hasn't missed a Tiger home game since 1948 and missed only two road games since 1969.

"The crowds weren't as large and there were only 11,000 students," Cocos said. "You had a lot of battle-scarred veterans there. When I got to college I had just turned 17, but I roomed with a guy who was 34 and was a veteran of the Battle of the Bulge. Veterans were working the concession stands. All the marching bands were male. There were very few cars on campus and no parking lots. You got to know people because you passed them every day on campus. You had to go to class there.

"It was fun watching the games, although it is not the caliber it is today when you have specialized people playing football on offense and defense. And they didn't have weight programs."

The first game that Cocos saw at Missouri was one for the scrapbook—the 1948 home opener against fourth-ranked SMU.

A record Missouri crowd—at that point—of 30,892 watched Heisman Trophy winner Doak Walker put on one great show, but in a losing effort, 20–14. He scored a rushing touchdown, caught a long scoring pass, kicked two extra points, and intercepted a pass.

"The only game we lost in 1948 was at Missouri," said Benton Musslewhite, an SMU back. "We got overconfident. We had a couple of bad breaks. It was a very, very shocking upset. It was a tragedy because we could have been undefeated, although we tied a game against TCU [Texas Christian University]."

"It was one of big games of that time and era," said Sauer. "SMU was one of top teams to come to Columbia…. That game was talked about for years. Every now and then you will still see it mentioned. Walker was the greatest player I ever saw in my limited career. And the crowd was capacity."

The following week Missouri beat Navy, 35–14, in Annapolis when Sauer intercepted two passes. The next day the Tigers got to meet Missouri's own President Harry Truman at the White House. After an 8–2 regular-season and runner-up finish to Oklahoma in the Big Seven, the Tigers received a berth in the Gator Bowl to play Clemson, which resulted in a bitter 24–23 loss.

The Clemson game started a string of three tough one-point losses over two seasons, including 35–34 to Ohio State in Columbus and 28–27 to SMU in Dallas to begin the 1949 season. But Missouri bounced back from those stinging defeats to win five straight before a loss to Oklahoma cost the Tigers a Big Seven title. The Gator Bowl was the postseason destination once again for a 7–3 regular season. Missouri's football team took its first plane trip in history—to Florida to play Maryland in Jacksonville on January 2, 1950, where the Tigers lost again, 20–7.

Nevertheless, Missouri took home nearly $180,000 over a two-year period for those bowl games, which was music to the frugal Faurot's ears.

"I have a picture of that, the picture in the paper," Sauer said. "The first airplane trip was on an Eastern Airlines *Constellation*. It was a rough trip down. We didn't fly at 46,000 feet. We flew much lower and hit a storm. Some of the guys got sick. I was a part of it. It was a thrill to ever do that."

In the late 1940s, Faurot's Tigers were second only to Wilkinson's Oklahoma Sooners in the Big Seven. Wilkinson actually had taken the option philosophies Faurot had taught him during World War II and used them to beat Faurot. Nevertheless, Faurot was held in great esteem by his players for his slow, easy-going approach, which was always consistent and fair. Faurot always liked to have meetings with his players to keep their time occupied and prevent them from "running the streets."

Missouri's 1949 backfield gets instructions from their coach prior to the January 2, 1950, Gator Bowl in Jacksonville, Florida. Kneeling left to right are: halfback Nick Carras, fullback Win Carter, and coach Don Faurot. Standing are: halfback Dick Braznell (left) and halfback Mike Ghnouly.

"He was a not a dynamic speaker like Knute Rockne or some-body like that," Sauer said. "His pregame talks were right to the point. He had terrific game preparations. We had regular quarter-back meetings to go over the game plan. We would meet in an area of Rothwell Gym.

"I always remember a guy named Denny Studer," Sauer con-tinued. "He would imitate Faurot at the chalkboard. Faurot walked in on him, but he took it in good sorts. Denny could throw his jaw out like Faurot did. Faurot had a prominent lower jaw. Faurot had lost two fingers off his right hand in a farm accident. And Denny would hold the chalk with his last two fingers and thumb."

Going to "The Spread"

Faurot was gradually balancing Missouri's athletic finances and enlarging Missouri's stadium to seat more than 30,000. However, Missouri's instate player pool began to dry up in the early 1950s. Still, it was Faurot's strategy to recruit as many Missouri players as possible and he doggedly stuck to it.

"He had great character," Tiger end Harold Burnine said of Faurot. "He stayed with what he believed in. He recruited and used Missouri players. He didn't go out of state much. Oklahoma went everywhere and a lot of others did, too. He stayed with his convictions. When I was freshman in 1950, he told us, 'Gentlemen, I want you to know why you are here. You work hard to get a degree and graduate from this university. You are a student first and an athlete second. We can turn the lights off out there to practice. Don't miss a class or a lab. If you don't approach it that way, if you don't graduate, you will find football pretty hard to digest.'"

Burnine actually had to go to the service—the Korean conflict—when his National Guard unit was called up. As a result, he didn't play until 1953. Missouri failed to post a winning season from 1950 to 1952. But with a scrambling freshman quarterback named Tony Scardino, who could throw on the run, Missouri was respectable. In 1951 and 1952, Faurot went to the spread offense that he had run as a player in the mid-1920s and coached at Kirksville later.

"The first time was against Bud Wilkinson (Oklahoma) in 1951," Faurot recalled in a 1982 interview in the *Fifth Down*, the Football Writers Association of America newsletter. "He played it with a four-man line, which is the way you should play it, I guess. He beat us 34–20…. And if I'd used the T (formation) we wouldn't have scored one (touchdown)."

Oklahoma was on its way to its sixth straight league title and featured two players in its line who would go on to win the Outland Trophy: Jim Weatherall at tackle (1951) and J.D. Roberts at guard (1953). Missouri was weak and inexperienced on the line, so it needed a little equalizer with a gimmicky offense.

"I had always had the spread in my repertoire, but hadn't used it too much, except at Kirksville a little bit," Faurot is quoted in *Fifth Down*. "When you get a sort of an 'underprivileged' team, something like that will give you a chance to make a game of it. Kansas had a real good team that year and we went over there and played them (a 41–28 loss). Without the spread, I bet they'd beat us, 48–0. After the game, I said, 'Well, old Faurot knows a little about offense—even if he doesn't know anything about defense.'"

Burnine: One Great Pass Catcher

Harold Burnine grew up in rural Missouri and was a three-sport star (basketball, track and football) at Richmond High School in Richmond, Missouri. He grew up idolizing Faurot's teams in the early 1940s, particularly the 1941 squad, which featured running backs Harry Ice, Bob Steuber, and Maurice Wade.

Little did he know he would be one of Faurot's great offensive stars in the 1950s and go on to a professional football career in 1956 and 1957 with the New York Giants and Philadelphia Eagles.

"In the 1940s, they put the Split T on the map," recalls Burnine, who is now retired and living in Tyler, Texas. "They had a great offense and led the nation in rushing offense. I remember they [Faurot and Ice] came into this little gym in Richmond, Missouri, when they were recruiting me. We had the gym at the grade school. I will never forget—we were practicing basketball. And Faurot was held in such high esteem. He and Harry Ice walked in there and everybody just stopped.

"He said, 'Son, how would you like to come down and represent your state university?' I tell you what, I was speechless. I said, 'That would be great, coach.' He said, 'You are a little skinny.' I never weighed more than 180 pounds.

"'We can put a little weight on him, don't you think, Ice?' Faurot asked his assistant coach.

"'He looks like he can play,' Ice replied.

"There were only two schools who recruited me—Missouri and Kansas," Burnine continued. "I talked to my dad. And he told me, 'If you go to Kansas, you better burn the bridges behind you.'"

Taking his father's advice, Burnine went to Missouri and enrolled as a freshman in 1950, but had to go into the service in January 1951. He didn't get on the field until the 1953 season.

Then, as a junior in 1954, he led the Big Seven in pass receptions with 22 catches for 405 yards. During the final game of the 1954 season, Maryland (and Faurot's old assistant coach Jim Tatum) put a 74–13 licking on the Tigers in College Park, Maryland.

"Maryland was all fired up," Burnine said. "And they had a great team. Jim Tatum, who Faurot taught, played the Split T. And boy, did he have material to run it! When we got on an airplane to go home, I wouldn't have blamed Coach Faurot if he had gone out to the Pacific Ocean to drop us. It was terrible. It was so embarrassing."

The skills Burnine displayed his junior season were just a glimpse of what he would do his final season at Missouri.

"I was a possession receiver in high school, college, and in the pros," Burnine said. "I did not have blinding speed. But I was fast enough to get it done there. I just knew how to jump into the creases."

He made up for a lack of blinding speed with a fast start. He was a hurdler in high school as well as a long and high jumper. He skipped running the hurdles in college because the MU track team had plenty of hurdlers. But he lettered in track at Missouri in the high jump and long jump for good reason.

"I went out for track, too, at Missouri, so I could work with the sprinters," Burnine said. "I would work on my start and get away from the line of scrimmage. It really helped. And it really worked for me up in the pros, where I was a wide receiver and only went one way. They only carried 33 on a squad and we had to return punts and kickoffs.

"At Missouri I played both ways. I was a cornerback on defense. I had a big guy, Al Portney, at defensive end, playing in front of me. He took about everything off me. I might have made a tackle or two."

For Burnine, the best and worst at Missouri were yet to come in 1955, his senior season. He is still the only Missouri receiver to lead the nation in pass receptions: He caught 44 passes for 594 yards despite double coverage. Burnine was named to a couple of All-America teams, but Missouri won only one game (1–9), Faurot's worst season at Missouri.

Burnine's senior season began with a 13–12 loss to eastern power Maryland. Missouri couldn't convert extra points in that game. The team went on to lose six games by seven or fewer points.

"I was a part of the worst season Faurot ever had," Burnine said. "I would be glad to trade all of that (All-America selections) for a better record. I want to emphasize this: we had several real fine passers that season...Jimmy Hunter got hurt against Michigan, but he came back the week we played at Colorado. We were not even supposed to be in the park with them. It was their homecoming game and we knocked them off (20–12). It was the only game we won that season. We could throw the ball. We had a big fullback, but we couldn't run wide. Defensively we were pretty good.

"What I will cherish most is making the All-Players' All-America team, which was selected by all the opponents we played. It was just the fact it was my peers. I will never forget that year. I felt like the priest at the Xerox machine. It's a miracle, instead of doing it by hand."

Although Burnine was not a baseball player, he did rub elbows with Missouri's legendary baseball coach John "Hi" Simmons who, as a football assistant, was a scout for the Missouri football team.

"He was super as a scout," Burnine said of Simmons. "He'd come back from scouting games and tell me, 'Look, don't try to run the post on this guy, run the corner.... He was really funny, too. I will never forget—he told me a story when he went out to Santa Clara to scout SMU in the 1947 opener. Missouri was playing

SMU the next week. He said, 'I was looking down through those eyeglasses. And SMU was running a flea flicker, the double reverse—they played with No. 37 (Doak Walker). It looked like a concession stand. I couldn't make out if he was making sandwiches or passing them out!'"

Faurot's Last Coaching Hurrah

Burnine was gone for Faurot's final season of 1956, which was much better (4–5–1) and topped off by a rousing season-ending 15–13 victory over Kansas. With only one winning season since his last bowl team of 1949, Faurot announced that the 1956 season would be his last. Missouri fans were growing weary of the losing seasons. Faurot would keep his athletic director duties for the next 10 years and hire a new head football coach.

Missouri lost to another of Coach Bud Wilkinson's OU juggernaut teams, 67–14, in the next-to-last game of the 1956 season. So, standing 3–5–1, a victory over Kansas in Columbia would be the emotional send-off Faurot needed to end on a good note.

In a tight struggle, the game was tied, 13–13, late. It appeared it would end in a tie when Kansas coach Chuck Mather misread the yard marker and believed the ball was on the 9-yard line instead of the four. He called a reverse and Missouri tackle Chuck Mehrer tackled the ball carrier in the end zone for a safety.

"They got the safety to beat KU at Columbia and they carried [Faurot] off the field," said Burnine, who was in pro football by then. "I was so thrilled he went out a winner. He was a guy you really put it on the line for."

Faurot moved solely into the athletic director's role and surveyed the country for his replacement. One of the coaches he considered was Bob Devaney, who was the line coach at Michigan State at the time. Devaney became coach at Wyoming and later went to Nebraska and won two national titles.

Faurot wound up hiring Frank Broyles, and then Dan Devine, but always had his finger on the program's purse strings.

Players carry Don Faurot off the field after his final game on the sidelines, a 15–13 win over Kansas on December 1, 1956, that gave him 101 career wins as Tigers coach.

"He was frugal to the extreme," remembers Russ Sloan, a Missouri end in the late 1950s. "We went to the Orange Bowl in 1959, and he found some clothing outfit store in Kansas City [where] he could buy, at a big discount, some black blazers and gray slacks which were wool. Here we are going to Miami in black wool blazers and gray pants. That was just the way he was. He grew up in an era which was extremely cost-conscious. And from an administrative standpoint, he ran a tight shop. But he was ethical to the core."

Faurot's Later Years

In 1972, five years after Faurot had relinquished his duties as MU athletic director to Dan Devine, the field at Memorial Stadium was named after Faurot. Although Memorial Stadium was officially listed as seating 62,000, crowds of more than 75,000 would watch games there by the end of the decade. Fans would spill over into the block "M" hillside in the north end zone and other temporary seating.

Before a home football game in 1972, 800 family and friends gathered to honor Faurot. His name was placed in a specially designed stone-and-wood gate at the northwest corner of the stadium that Faurot had coddled and nurtured into a big-time structure.

Devine, who also served as Missouri's head football coach from 1958 to 1970 and who succeeded Faurot as athletic director in 1967, had left Missouri to coach the Green Bay Packers in January 1971. But Devine wrote a letter that was read at the 1972 gathering:

> The thing that stands out more than any other in our relationship is the fact that Don sincerely and honestly wanted me to succeed. This may sound like a very simple thing, but in so many cases it is not true. A former coach becomes an administrator and subconsciously, he doesn't want his successor to have great success which might overshadow his own considerable accomplishments. Not Faurot. He was very unselfish and was always my strongest supporter and best friend.
>
> When the chips were down you could always depend on Faurot. He had—and still has—one of the greatest football minds in the country. A great man in all ways.

Faurot was in his 70s at the time of his retirement and remained fit enough to play golf into his 80s. He also did color commentary for Tigers games and helped assemble all-star squads for the Blue-Gray and Senior Bowl games. He served as secretary for the Missouri Sports Hall of Fame and executive secretary of the Missouri Senior Golf Association. While in his 80s, Faurot directed senior golf groups to Hawaii, and commented, "That's the only job I ever had that was better than coaching."

Faurot would appear in the Missouri football press box and sit often next to the late Bob Broeg, columnist for the *St. Louis Post-Dispatch*.

"I loved Don Faurot, he was such a great guy," said Dave Hart, Missouri athletic director from 1978 to 1986. "He had an office and would come in almost every day."

When he died on October 19, 1995, at the age of 93, Missouri had lost a favorite son. But he had left a sort of symmetrical and symbolic token of his presence on Faurot Field shortly before his death in 1995. In 1926, Faurot, a graduate student at the time, helped lay sod prior to the opening of Memorial Stadium. Seventy years later, he laid the final piece of sod as Missouri returned to natural grass after 10 years of the often-criticized OmniTurf.

"Don Faurot was a top-notch person," said Wayne Duke, the former commissioner of both the Big Eight and Big Ten conferences. "I said when he died [that] if there were more Don Faurots in the college athletic business, we would be so much better off."

chapter 2
Transition Years

"We were all pretty stunned when [Frank Broyles] left…. He wanted to recruit other places. He didn't think there was great talent in [Missouri]. He felt that his hands were tied and he was going to move on."

—Phil Snowden

Broyles Had Tough Approach

Missouri's players were in for a dramatic change of culture when they reported for spring drills in 1957 under first-time head coach Frank Broyles. Broyles, a Southerner, had coached and played under Georgia Tech's Bobby Dodd, whose approach to football was quite different from Don Faurot's.

While Faurot coached wide-open and innovative offenses and had a less-stressful approach to conditioning, Broyles was going to emphasize defense, conservative offense, the kicking game, and repetition in drills to the point of… well, let Russ Sloan, an end on the 1957 team, tell you.

"I wrote coach Broyles a letter," Sloan recalled. "And I told him, 'The only difference between you and Bear Bryant is you kept us on campus.'"

Sloan's reference was to the famous preseason camp that Bryant, prior to his first season as head coach at Texas A&M in 1954, ran in Junction, Texas, away from the Aggie campus.

That camp was so tough, it led to the book *The Junction Boys*, which was later made into an ESPN movie depicting the ornery and unyielding Bear. Under the sweltering and unrelenting conditions of Junction, Bryant tried to rid the dead weight that he believed he had inherited when he arrived at Texas A&M.

"The conditioning (at Missouri) liked to have killed us," said Merv Johnson, who was a Missouri senior during the 1957 season. "All the running and agility-type activity we hadn't done. We were trimming guys down weight-wise. It was really tough…but we made it through it and were a decent team. It was very different. Bobby Dodd's teams would win with great defense and a great kicking game. They would win the close ones. They would quick kick (on third down) and we never did that under Faurot. That was a huge weapon with those teams. That philosophy was totally different."

In the spring and fall of 1957, the Bear's presence was felt because two of Broyles's assistant coaches, Jerry Claiborne and Jim Mackenzie, had played for the Bear at Kentucky several years earlier.

"We were losing eight, nine, 10 guys a day," Sloan said of the Mizzou camps during the spring and summer of 1957. "We had 100 freshmen on the freshman team and we had nine of us left four years later.

"Going into that spring we had 120, how many were walking at the end?" Sloan added. "I just know it was a revolving door both in spring ball and before the season. He replicated what they did at Texas A&M. Broyles was a phenomenal coach. It was a whole different gear up from the way it had been conducted. At the end of lot of practices, Broyles would have Cokes all poured. He would say, 'I love you all.' He worked our butts off. And he would reward us with a Coke. Broyles was the epitome of organization and was a great motivator. He demanded 100 percent."

Bear's 1957 Aggie team—his last at the school before taking the Alabama job—actually beat Broyles's Tigers, 28–0, in Columbia. In *The Razorbacks: A Story of Arkansas Football,* by Orville Henry and Jim Bailey, Broyles recalled that before the game, Bear commented to him that Missouri had no athletes. That was surely one of the reasons Broyles didn't stick around longer than a year to use Faurot's homegrown "Show-Me" State recruits.

Broyles Recruits Mike Shannon

One of Broyles's top recruits was Mike Shannon, who went on to star for the St. Louis Baseball Cardinals (1962–1970) and soon thereafter became a radio broadcaster for the professional baseball club where he has remained ever since.

Shannon was recruited and signed to a football scholarship by Broyles, Missouri's head football coach for one season in 1957.

Broyles said he went to Shannon's home in the St. Louis area to recruit the standout quarterback from St. Louis Christian Brothers College (CBC) High School.

"It was a hot day," Broyles recalled of the recruiting trip. "His father was sitting in a chair and was wearing just an undershirt. I walked in and he immediately said, 'Want a beer?'"

Trying to warm up to the recruit's dad, the teetotaler Broyles accepted the beer. But the suds never crossed his mouth. When Shannon's father wasn't looking, Broyles disposed of the beer drop by drop in the nearest container that he could find.

"I knew I did something with it," recalled Broyles in December 2007, about 50 years later. "I saw Mike Shannon down in Augusta recently, and he reminded me I poured it in a potted plant.

"I will never forget his father watching my lips as I talked," Broyles said. "He had never heard someone talk like I did with a Georgia drawl."

Broyles won the recruiting war, but was off to Arkansas before Shannon could play varsity football for Missouri. Shannon attended Missouri as a freshman in 1957, but in those days freshmen weren't eligible for varsity competition. Shannon opted for a better-paying professional baseball career (compared to professional football in those days) and eventually became the baseball Cardinals' starting right fielder and later the third baseman.

"He always says, if I would have stayed, he would have stayed," Broyles said. "And he says he would have won the Heisman."

For a season, at least, it was Broyles's way or no way. And he recruited the first two African American football players to get scholarships at Missouri, halfbacks Norris Stevenson from Vashon High school in St. Louis and Mel West from Jefferson City High School in Jefferson City, Missouri. The two were freshmen in the fall of 1957, didn't play for the varsity, and wouldn't be factors until the Dan Devine era.

But they weren't scared off, either, by what was going on under Broyles's rule.

"Maybe [Broyles] thought the only way we could compete was to practice harder and be tougher," said Phil Snowden, who was a sophomore quarterback in 1957. "There was some logic to it. But how far do you go? How many wind sprints and drills do you do? The linemen had almost some cruel and unusual punishment. The backs were a little luckier. [The coaches] probably went over the top."

Snowden, a standout quarterback from North Kansas City (Missouri) High School, said Broyles didn't dedicate a lot of time to offense.

"I really liked him and several people on the staff," Snowden said of Broyles. "He and I had a good relationship and by the third game, I was starting offensively and defensively…. We didn't spend a huge amount of time on offense…. We didn't throw it very much. We didn't work on it. We did not have many plays. We ran a tight set."

The Game that the Quarterback Ran

Missouri finished Broyles's only season in Columbia with a nondescript 5−4−1 record. The Tigers dropped their final three games to Oklahoma, Kansas State, and Kansas after winning five of their first seven games (they lost to Texas A&M and tied Vanderbilt).

Snowden remembers a remarkable mid-season, come-from-behind 14−13 victory over Nebraska in Columbia during which he improvised on offense.

"Nebraska wasn't a great team," Snowden said. "We were behind 13−0 and in the last half we were not getting anything going. I started calling plays in the huddle [that] we didn't have. I was making up plays like 'sandlot,' telling Russ Sloan and others, 'You do this and we are going to do this.' We moved and scored a couple of touchdowns. Several plays were made-up plays. I was just drawing a line in the sand.

"I was worried about it," Snowden continued. "You don't do crazy things like calling your own plays. When we got through, Hank Kuhlmann scored on a pretty good run and we won the game after we kicked the extra point. Afterward, not a word was said by any coach. I thought Broyles would come down on me and say, 'What's that play? Where did you come up with that?' We went around and did our normal business. I never did bring it up. He never brought it up. I thought it was better for me to keep quiet and not say anything. Some of the players talked about it at times. And Sloan and I talked about it."

Missouri won the next week at Colorado, 9–6. Then came the three-game tailspin to end the season and ultimately Broyles's brief tenure at Columbia. Snowden looked back to the preseason camp as a reason why the Tigers struggled down the stretch.

"I remember the Oklahoma game, at the end of the third quarter, I just thought the game was over, it can't go any longer than this," Snowden said of a 39–14 loss to the powerful Sooners. "I think I played 50 minutes. I was pretty skinny and played offense and defense and was fairly young for my class. It wore on you.

"It was so dang hot in the (preseason) camp. We lost a lot of weight.... I really think because of that, we were worn out toward end of year and didn't play very well. We only had 16, 17 guys playing much. Some of us were averaging in the high 40s, low 50s [minutes]. We had to go both ways."

Broyles's Departure to Arkansas

Sloan remembers Broyles saying at the banquet following the 1957 season that "I will be here all as long as you want." But three days later, Broyles departed for Arkansas, where he became a legend in the Southwest Conference and his Razorbacks a major challenge to Darrell Royal's Texas Longhorns for nearly two decades.

"We knew he was a great coach, and the future looked bright," Sloan said. "I think maybe he thought that Oklahoma was head and shoulders above us competitively. He went to Arkansas, where he had a free hand to build a program. There wasn't that dominance in the SWC by one team, that there was in our conference."

Much of Broyles's departure seemed to whirl around the differences he had with the in-state recruiting philosophy that Faurot had long espoused and continued to demand as Missouri's athletic director.

"We were all pretty stunned when [he] left," Snowden said. "I never talked to Broyles about it, but the word was Faurot was running a tight ship and he didn't like Missouri spending lots of money. He didn't want to recruit out of state. He wanted to win with Missouri guys. Broyles had other ideas. He wanted to recruit other places. He didn't think there was great talent in the state. He felt that his hands were tied and he was going to move on."

Merv Johnson, who was a graduate assistant coach on Broyles's 1958 and 1959 Razorback teams, said Broyles had always wanted the Arkansas job. And Sloan credits Broyles for putting together the nucleus for Devine's near brush with the national championship in 1960. In any event, Devine was a return to an offensive-minded head coach, albeit still conservative.

"[Devine assistants] Al Onofrio and Clay Cooper ran the defense," Johnson said. "Dan spent a lot more time on offense, as Faurot did. Dan wanted to move the ball up the field and eat up the clock. Don liked to spread it out like he did with Tony Scardino. He wanted to move the chains with the passing and running game. Devine was much more run-oriented."

The Devine Era Begins

Snowden said when Devine, a Minnesota native, came in from Arizona State, Faurot realized "they have some new ideas and 'maybe I am going to loosen up and or I will not have me a coach.' He never told me that. Devine didn't tell me. That was the word traveling. Devine had more of a free rein. He had ties in Michigan and in Chicago and recruited good players out of that area as well as recruiting Missouri."

Missouri started 1–3 under Devine, including a 12–8 opening loss to Vanderbilt and a stinging 32–19 home loss to No. 18 SMU in the fourth game of the season. The Mustangs rallied to score all 32 points in the second half. The Tigers committed six turnovers in that game.

"We got off to a slow start," Snowden said of the 1958 season. "It was a brand-new offense and completely brand-new defense. It was harder to adjust on defense. We ran more of a multiple

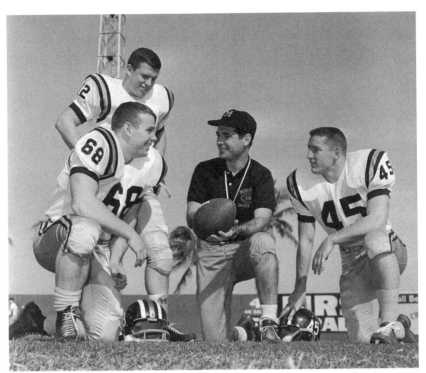

New coach Dan Devine, shown here with (from left to right) guard Paul Henley, quarterback Ron Taylor, and halfback Donnie Smith, took over the Tigers in 1958 after Frank Broyles served as Missouri's coach for just one season.

offense, a little bit of the single wing he ran down at Arizona State, and we did some belly series. Then we got into the sweep stuff and it evolved into student body right and left, especially in 1960. It was an evolving process.

"The one big change from a defensive back's standpoint [was that] we were running a complete zone—linebacker and deep backs—under Broyles," Snowden added. "We got to the point we were pretty good at it. We just covered an area. Even though we did not have great speed and talent, at one time we ranked among the top 10, 12 in the nation under Broyles [in pass defense]. When Devine came in, his assistant [Tom Fletcher] had experience in the pros where they ran a lot of man-to-man coverage. We were switching off and it was very complicated. We just didn't adjust. We didn't have a lot of speed. If you can't stay with someone one-on-one, that's [the] toughest position, playing somebody man-to-man."

That was apparent in the second half of the SMU game. Had Missouri not scored a touchdown with 36 seconds remaining to beat Idaho, 14–10, in the second game of the season, the Tigers would have started 0–4.

A pivotal game that season was at Kansas State, a week after the second-half collapse against SMU. Standing 1–3, Missouri beat the Wildcats, 32–8, with a 388-yard offensive day. It was the beginning of a four-game winning streak.

"It was one of those games going out to Kansas State. It was a beautiful afternoon and everything we did clicked, "Snowden remembers. "Everyone was working and knew exactly what to do. I was having one of these really good days throwing the ball. Everything I threw was right on target. It seemed like one of the easiest victories we ever had."

Snowden pinpoints another turning point for Devine at Missouri that came three weeks later. This one involved his own personal comeback following an injury.

"We were playing Colorado and we were behind 9–0 going into the second half," Snowden recalls. "I had gotten hurt two weeks before against Iowa State. I had broken some bone in my backside. I was still in the hospital the next week when we played Nebraska. On the Monday after that game, I got out. We were getting ready to play Colorado. But I couldn't walk. By Wednesday, I could. They made a plastic cast. Our trainer Fred Wappel formed it, thinking in the next couple of games I could wear the cast on my back."

Snowden warmed up before the Colorado game, jogged a little bit, and suited up. But he didn't play in the first half and the MU offense was anemic.

"Devine at half asked me, 'Want to try this [the cast]?'" Snowden recalled. "'Make sure you don't run the ball,' Devine told me. 'Do the minimal amount and see if we can generate some offense.' We scored five times in 11 minutes and I ran for a couple and passed for two. Out of that I was selected the Associated Press back of the week. Everything fell into place. I scored on a long run. And Devine just was shaking his head on the sidelines."

The modest four-game Mizzou winning streak ended the next week at Oklahoma, 39–0, as the Sooner powerhouse overwhelmed the Tigers. But even after that game, Sloan said, Devine vowed to the seniors that the return trip two years later to Norman, Oklahoma, would be different. And it would be.

In the 1958 season finale, Kansas came into Columbia and pulled out a 13–13 tie when it scored on an 80-yard pass play with 18 seconds remaining. Only a blocked extra point kept Missouri from defeat. It was the third straight game between the two teams to come down to the final minute.

"We shouldn't have tied [Kansas]," Snowden said. "We didn't have the right personnel on the field at the end of game when they hit that long pass."

It was one of the few times that would happen during the Devine era at Missouri. A golden period was about to begin.

chapter 3
Orange Bowl Years

"We were optimistic, but never were dreaming we would almost run the table…. We never dreamed we would be that close to a national championship. It would have been huge."

—Merv Johnson,
remembering the
1960 Missouri Tigers

The 1959 season, Devine's second at Missouri, started with much anticipation. But it also suffered from a dulling, consistent theme—losing the opener. In Devine's first season, the Tigers dropped their opener to Vanderbilt. And his second year began with a 19–8 loss to Penn State.

The Tigers' loss to the Nittany Lions in Columbia was the 12th straight time the Tigers had failed to win their opener. Since Don Faurot's Tigers had beaten St. Louis University in 1947, Missouri had a 0–11–1 record in openers. Only Frank Broyles's 7–7 tie against Vanderbilt in the 1957 opener kept it from being a complete whitewash.

But Missouri would overcome that opening loss and head to its first bowl game since the 1950 Gator Bowl.

In the 1959 opener, Missouri's secondary was scorched by the skilled passing of Penn State's Richie Lucas. Unbelievably, he was one of five top college quarterbacks the Tigers would face during the course of the 1959 season. The others were Kansas's John Hadl, SMU's Don Meredith, Air Force's Richie Mayo, and Georgia's Fran Tarkenton, the latter in the Orange Bowl.

"All five were mentioned as preseason All-Americans," Missouri end Russ Sloan said. "I don't think it has likely been replicated that one team has faced that many great passers in one season."

Winning at Michigan

After the loss to Penn State, Devine's first big Missouri road victory came in the second game of the 1959 season—a thrilling 20–15 victory over Michigan in Bump Elliott's first game as the Wolverines' head coach.

Unexpectedly, Bob Haas—a 6-foot, 181-pound senior reserve quarterback from Northeast High School in Kansas City—became the Tigers' hero. Haas ran the ball over from one yard out with three seconds remaining, culminating a 78-yard drive when he completed three clutch passes. A 33-yard field goal had given Michigan a 15–14 lead with 2:48 remaining.

"You won the game for us," Devine told Haas, reported the *St. Louis Post-Dispatch*. "That was the greatest clutch performance I have ever seen, the greatest."

Starting quarterback Phil Snowden had gone out in favor of Haas, who also picked off two of four Missouri interceptions against Michigan. Because of the limited substitution rule in that era, Haas had to stay in the game to play quarterback. Haas was also a punter and a baseball player. His son later played for the Detroit Tigers.

"Phil Snowden was very tough, overall a good athlete and a good basketball player, a good, bright student of game," Sloan said. "But Haas was the better of the two defensively.... That was a phenomenal win. I remember after we won that we went though a very long tunnel under the stands and the door was locked to our locker room. Coach Devine said, 'Break it down.'"

West, Stevenson: Mizzou's Jackie Robinsons

Mel West and Norris Stevenson, the Tigers' first African American players, had broken into the Missouri scene in 1958. West was the Tigers' leading rusher as a sophomore with 642 yards and a 4.8 yards-per-carry average. He also led the Tigers in rushing in 1959 and 1960 with similar rushing averages. Stevenson, who caught a pivotal 39-yard scoring pass against Air Force in 1959, added a second big-time running pass-catching threat and could run the 100-yard dash in 10 seconds flat.

"To me, they epitomized the very way, the determination and qualities Jackie Robinson took to Major League Baseball," Sloan said. "They were our Jackie Robinsons, in terms of character, composure, and talent."

Sloan remembers one ugly racial incident in 1958, Devine's first season, when the Tigers traveled to Texas A&M to play the Aggies in early October. "The hotel there fed all of our kids in a private dining area. But I don't think they [the African American players] were allowed in the public restaurant; they wouldn't serve blacks. I remember a group of us there got up and walked out. We weren't requested to do it. It was within our ranks."

Racism ultimately would rear its head again after the Tigers played Georgia in the 1960 Orange Bowl following the 1959 season.

"I know one thing, a decision Dan Devine regrets," Snowden said. "I know he apologized afterward. When we were at the Orange Bowl, we got to go to a country club and have a big party after the game. It was a real nice place. But they wouldn't let Mel West and Norris Stevenson come to the country club. They told them, 'You can't come.' The rest of the players didn't know about it. [Devine] had to make the decision to let the rest of the team in. He made the decision to let the rest come in. Later, I know, he regretted tremendously making that decision…. He felt real bad about it."

Back on the field, in 1959 two weeks after the big Michigan win, the Tigers lost to SMU in Dallas, 23–2, when Meredith had a big game. West ran 15 times for 69 yards, but the Tigers suffered three interceptions. Still, SMU's head coach saw something in West that was developing despite a 2–2 Tiger start that season.

"Missouri has a rugged ball club and will win lots of games before the season is over," SMU coach Bill Meek said. "Mel West was especially outstanding for the Tigers. We knew from our game with Missouri last year and our scout reports this season that he is one of the best ball carriers we would face this year. I think it was his greatness and our players' weakness that resulted in several of his gains. Several times when we had him trapped apparently, he would outmaneuver our boys and pick up several additional yards."

Sending the Ends, Claiming the Orange Bowl Berth

Missouri's defensive architect, Al Onofrio, decided to rush ends Danny LaRose and Russ Sloan for the first time against Air Force quarterback Richie Mayo in the eighth game of the 1959 season.

Sloan said the Air Force team was one of the cockiest he had ever played against. Missouri won, 13–0.

"I would imagine all service academies have a tremendous amount of pride," Sloan said. "But it was hard to differentiate between pride and cockiness. They took the opening kickoff and made three or four quick first downs. Then we shut them down…I just think that we needed to get more rush on the passer."

Missouri blanked Kansas State, 26–0, the next week to post its fourth shutout of the season—the most shutouts by a Missouri club since Faurot's 1941 Tiger team hurled five of them.

The rugged rush end was a staple of Missouri's defenses under Devine, where All-Conference and All-American players were commonplace, starting with Sloan and LaRose, then Conrad Hitchler and George Seals. As a sophomore in 1958, LaRose had shown his potential from end when he blocked two punts against Vanderbilt, one out of the end zone for a safety.

"I think the defense was largely Al's," Sloan said. "Al was my end coach. And I loved Onofrio. Whatever success I had, I attribute to all the coaches. Al, in particular, was a huge asset to me. Within Devine's breakdown of responsibilities, Al really had to run the defense. From the day he let LaRose and I loose on Air Force, [it] worked well. Danny was All-Conference in 1958 and I was All-Conference in 1959. Danny [LaRose] was All-American in 1960 and Hitchler was All-Conference and All-American. We went through an era when Missouri ends got a lot of recognition."

A lesser-known Missouri defensive end would play a big part in the 1959 regular-season-ending 13–9 victory over Hadl and the Jayhawks in Lawrence. That game turned out to be the deciding game for the Orange Bowl berth in Miami.

Oklahoma won the 1959 Big Seven championship but because the Sooners had been to the Orange Bowl the two previous seasons, the Miami-based game preferred another league team. Iowa State, Missouri, and Kansas were tied for second going into the final week of play. Oklahoma beat Iowa State to eliminate the Cyclones. Thus, the Missouri-KU winner would go to Miami.

Missouri right end Dale Pidcock, a 6'3", 200-pound senior from St. Louis, tripped up Hadl on a screen pass short of the goal on a fourth-down play in the closing minutes of victory over the Jayhawks and preserved Missouri's four-point victory.

Missouri: A Big Underdog

The Tigers were decided underdogs in their first bowl game in more than a decade. Entering the Orange Bowl with a 6–4 record and a modest three-game winning streak, No. 18 Missouri faced a fifth-ranked Georgia team that had posted a one-loss season.

"We know we are facing a great team," Devine said. "Georgia won the Southeastern Conference. And it is one of three teams from that league which finished among the nation's top five. Furthermore, four other SEC teams, aside from Georgia, earned bowl bids this year, so they proved themselves against the best."

Tarkenton, who later would star for the Minnesota Vikings, passed for two touchdowns against the Tigers. But the final score—Georgia 14, Missouri 0—was deceptive. The Tigers had their chances and blew them with three interceptions. They learned, however, what it took to win on the national stage when they returned to Miami a year later.

"We dramatically changed our offense for that one game," Snowden said. "We ran our split end, Russ Sloan, left. We should have done that when he first came in. Russ did not have great speed, but he was elusive. If you would get the ball close to him, he could catch it. We had a pretty darn good game on offense. I really had a percentage advantage and more passing yards than Tarkenton did. But we didn't win the game. If we had run that offense all season, we probably would have won two or three more games that season. We may not have beaten Oklahoma or Penn State. But everybody else we would have stayed right with."

Sloan had six receptions against Georgia.

"We out-played Georgia that day," Sloan said. "Tarkenton probably was the difference. I caught six passes that day. I was wide open at the 5 and Snowden threw eight yards behind me and a guy intercepted it. We were better than Georgia, but we didn't get it done. We were probably one year away from greatness."

Devine's postmortem summed up Missouri's season of trying to stop hot quarterbacks during 1959.

"Tarkenton was an excellent quarterback but not the passer Don Meredith is," Devine said. "He's more like Richie Lucas of Penn State in his running and passing. We planned on rushing the passer. The two touchdowns they got came when their passer got away from our rushing."

Devine Changes the Culture

Devine was definitely changing the culture at Missouri. In 1960, the Tigers would win the newly expanded Big Eight Conference—which had just added Oklahoma State—contend for the national championship, and return to Miami and win the first bowl game in school history.

It would take an asterisk to wipe out an on-the-field loss to Kansas, but Missouri would finish with 11 victories for the first time in the 20th century.

"We were optimistic, but never were dreaming we would almost run the table," said former Missouri player Merv Johnson, an assistant on Devine's staff in 1960 and 1961. "We had a great group of seniors and a quality junior class and became a heck of a football team. We stubbed our toe against KU. We never dreamed we would be that close to a national championship. It would have been huge."

The Tigers, with quarterback Ron Taylor at the controls, were running the power sweep with aplomb with West, Stevenson, and Donnie Smith. Missouri's offensive and defensive lines were littered with stars.

"We had a great year," Johnson continued. "Danny LaRose was a big guy, athletic and our punter. He did it all. Eddie Blaine was a great lineman. Conrad Hitchler was older and had come back from the Marines."

Missouri needed to win its first opener since 1947 and did it with a smashing 20–0 victory over SMU in Columbia, which left little doubt to the shell-shocked Mustangs that this Missouri team was going places.

"Missouri is a good, sound team," said SMU back Glynn Gregory after the game. "And they play as a team. They hit hard and ought to go a long way."

Against the Mustangs, the Tigers turned two intercepted passes and a fumble into touchdown drives. Taylor threw only five passes and completed four. But during the entire season, Taylor would attempt only 44 passes and complete 23 of them. With Missouri's defense and punishing running game, Devine believed there was little reason to pass.

"These guys were never down," Taylor said of his linemen. "Our rushing was tremendous. And when linemen knock down as many passes as ours did, they can't beat you."

The Tigers racked up victories week after week and moved steadily up in the rankings after beating Air Force, 34–8, in Denver to begin a season with four straight wins for the first time since 1924. Devine got the game ball for the Air Force contest. The Tigers led 27–0 at halftime as Mayo was shut down. Donnie Smith raced 90 yards down the sideline for Tigers' third touchdown, setting Mizzou's then-record for the longest punt return.

The next week, Missouri crushed Kansas State, 45–0, for its first 5–0 start since 1905. Smith had three touchdown runs. Missouri carried the ball 80 times to Kansas State's 16 times. Kansas State Coach Doug Weaver's team managed only 11 yards rushing—one yard short of a Tigers record. Kansas State couldn't stop Missouri's power playoff tackle. Victories over Nebraska and Colorado vaulted Missouri into the No. 2 ranking nationally heading into the long-awaited November 12 game at Oklahoma.

It was the return match that Devine had talked about after the 1958 loss in Norman.

The Sooners were having a down year in 1960, but had still won or tied for the previous 14 conference titles. And the Tigers had not won in Norman in 24 years. No league team had won there since Nebraska had pulled off the trick in 1942.

Missouri fell behind early when it gave up its first rushing touchdown of the season on the fourth play of the game. The Sooners couldn't stop MU's power game, either.

Smith scored three times rushing and Norris Stevenson scored twice on runs of 77 and 60 yards.

One unidentified Sooner defender was weary of watching Stevenson run that day when Missouri posted a 41–19 victory: "He had a nice [rear end], because that's all I saw all day."

Falling from No. 1

The OU victory vaulted Missouri to a No. 1 ranking in the country for the first time in school history going into the season-ending game against Kansas in Columbia. Both teams were unbeaten in Big Eight play and a showdown for the title was set.

"That week they printed out T-shirts with 'AHAB' on it," remembers Bill Tobin, who was a sophomore on the Tiger team. "All the students were wearing them when they went to class. It stood for 'All Hawks Are Bastards.' We would be the No. 1 team. All we had to do was beat Kansas. It didn't work out that way."

Before 43,000 fans, KU upset Missouri, 23–7. Behind offensive stars Bert Coan, John Hadl, and Curtis McClinton, the Jayhawks got ahead and stayed there in what was one of the bitterest defeats in Missouri history.

"Devine was much more run-oriented," Merv Johnson said. "That probably hurt us in the Kansas game. We got behind and couldn't throw it."

Missouri did not make a first down until 9:06 remained in the third quarter and gained only 61 yards on the ground. The score was 0–0 at halftime, but KU scored 10 points in the third quarter and 13 in the fourth. Missouri's only score was a 17–yard pass from Taylor to West in the fourth quarter. After trailing 17–7, Missouri fumbled three times

"It was one of those days in which we did all the things—bad ones—we hadn't done all year," Devine said.

Later Kansas was stripped of the victory because of the use of Coan, who was ineligible. The Jayhawks stayed home during bowl season and Missouri dropped in the polls from No. 1 to No. 5 after the loss. Because the polls were final before the bowl games, Missouri had no shot at the national title.

Missouri's First Bowl Victory

The Tigers had to regroup to play Navy and Heisman Trophy–winning running back Joe Bellino. It was very important to Devine for Missouri to break a seven-game postseason losing streak dating back to 1924, and he was confident the Tigers would bounce back.

"We have about the same kids we had last year, but we are much better than the club that lost in the Orange Bowl last New Year's Day to Georgia," Devine told *The Miami News*. "We have a little more team speed, a little more experience and a little more all-round ability. The sophomores and juniors you saw last year simply have developed and are better players."

The Orange Bowl setting was still a classic one for Missouri to show it was a national power under Devine.

"Service academies had great teams in those days," said Bill Tobin, who kicked three extra points after the Tigers' three touchdowns. "President-elect John Kennedy was in the audience. It was neat to play in front of the President. He was not in office yet. But he and Jackie were at the game. He, of course, was rooting for Navy."

Kansas fans even added to the scenery in Miami.

"Some of the Kansas big cigars rented a plane, with the score KU 23–7 on the trailer," said Wayne Duke, who worked at the NCAA at the time, but later became the Big Eight

Missouri quarterback Ronald Taylor hurdles Navy defenders in the third quarter of the 1961 Orange Bowl. The Tigers prevailed 21–14 and earned their first bowl victory.

commissioner. "And they flew it over the stadium. There was a lot of ill feeling."

Missouri stacked an eight-man line against the Heisman Trophy winner. Bellino was held to four yards rushing, and Navy minus 8 yards rushing as a team, in Missouri's 21–14 victory.

"We just dared them to throw that day," Merv Johnson said. "We had some athletic people and Andy Russell (linebacker, with two interceptions in that game) was a great player."

The Tigers, who pounded out 296 yards rushing, never let Bellino get into the open field, running the ball. He did have a 27-yard touchdown reception in the fourth quarter. Missouri stunted at the line of scrimmage and clogged Bellino's running lanes without getting hurt on the pass.

"I know Bellino would be a lot tougher downfield," Missouri tackle Ed Blaine said. "But we were able to stop him in the line, where he couldn't have much lateral movement."

Missouri fans could play the what-if game after beating No. 4 Navy in the Orange Bowl. What if the polls had been decided after the bowls? Even with the loss to Kansas, the Tigers could have wound up No. 1. Top-ranked Minnesota lost to Washington in the Rose Bowl, No. 2 Mississippi slipped past unranked Rice in the Sugar Bowl, and No. 3 Iowa did not play in a bowl game.

"The game was not as close as the score," Russ Sloan said of Missouri's victory over Navy. "That was the greatest team Missouri has ever had."

chapter 4
Devine in the 1960s

"[Dan Devine] was the most different coach I have ever been around, and I am sure he was a mystery to a lot of us…. We were very sound fundamentally, very well prepared, and didn't beat ourselves. He was a far, far different coach than Frank Broyles and Don Faurot."

—Russ Sloan

Out of the Decade's Best Programs

Under Coach Dan Devine, Missouri was the only team in major college football to not lose more than three games in a season during the 1960s. The Tigers won 75 percent of their regular-season games, excluding a forfeit from Kansas.

Toss in four 1960s bowl victories over Navy, Georgia Tech, Florida, and Alabama and a loss to Penn State (five games that the NCAA doesn't compute in its decade rankings) and Mizzou's percentage would even be higher.

From 1960 to 1969, Missouri's worst record was 6–3–1 twice, in 1964 and 1966. In the 1960s, Devine took the Tigers to five bowls (Orange twice, Sugar, Gator, and Bluebonnet). The Tigers probably could have gone to one after every season, but schools often turned down bowl invitations in that era.

Often aloof, Devine was a perfectionist, somewhat eccentric, and always a control freak in regards to his players and game preparations. High above the Missouri practice fields in his tower, Devine ruled with his clipboard and stern looks. But he delegated authority to several very competent assistant coaches to carry out his wishes and was a great organizer of his staff.

Devine ran Missouri like Mizzou Corp. Over the years, the Devine coaching tree included Hank Kuhlmann, Vince Tobin, Bill Tobin, Rollie Dotsch, Merv Johnson, Carl Reese, Johnny Roland, Al Onofrio, Clay Cooper, John Kadlec, and many others. Kuhlmann, Dotsch, and the Tobins all went into the professional ranks as coaches and/or front-office personnel. Johnson and Reese became top-notch college assistants. Johnny Roland played for Devine and later became an NFL star and assistant coach.

"Hank Kuhlmann, Johnny, and Vince and I were involved in [the] NFL for many, many years," said Bill Tobin, MU's star running back in the 1962 Bluebonnet Bowl victory over Georgia Tech. "That's the type of people he had. He didn't bring in any bums. He didn't bring in people who couldn't make the grade in the class-room, do their own work, and fulfill a commitment. He drafted stability and ability."

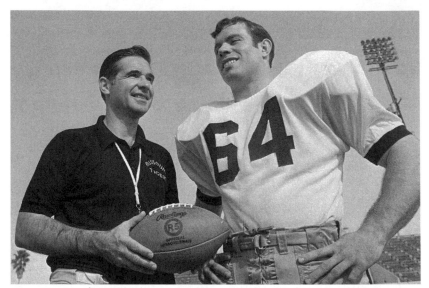

Dan Devine (pictured here with team captain Carl Garber prior to the 1968 Gator Bowl) and his Missouri Tigers were the only college football program in the nation to not lose more than three games in a season during the 1960s.

Cooper, Onofrio, and Kadlec remained at Devine's side and stayed at Missouri even after Devine left for Green Bay. Cooper and Onofrio fashioned one of the most aggressive defenses in college football during the 1960s.

"I think [Devine] was ahead of his time," Reese said. "A lot of that was Clay Cooper and Al Onofrio. They were no-nonsense and hustle and made you get with it. They played an eight-man front with the ends and outside backs coming up.... Sometimes they would have nine people committed to the run and put the two cornerbacks on islands. It was a great pass rush. Other teams were not doing it."

Several of Devine's players at Missouri also filtered into the coaching ranks of the NFL and big-time college football.

Jim Johnson, current defensive coordinator for the Philadelphia Eagles, played for Missouri as a quarterback in the early 1960s. Former Michigan coach Lloyd Carr was on the Tigers roster in the mid-1960s before transferring to Northern Michigan University.

Former Colorado head football coaches Bill McCartney and Gary Barnett, who also was head coach at Northwestern University, both played at Missouri. Woody Widenhofer, who later coached Pittsburgh's "Steel Curtain" defense and returned as head coach of the Tigers in 1985, played for Devine at MU. And Francis Peay, a Missouri All-American offensive tackle in 1965, was later head coach at Northwestern.

"He always surrounded himself with excellent coaches, all great coaches," said Reese, who remained as a Missouri graduate assistant coach in the mid-1960s after his playing days.

But there was much, much more to Devine than just good assistant coaches and top-flight players. He was a complex individual, a private man, and a cleanliness freak.

Devine was the product of a family of eight children growing up in Minnesota. When his father became ill and had trouble making ends meet, the family had to be broken up and sent to live at relatives' homes. Devine had no control then. But as a head football coach he did.

"Since I have been in coaching business 39 years, I keep looking at Devine and what he brought to the table and why he was a winner," Reese said. "He was an interesting guy. He was a psychologist way before you would talk about it. He would phrase things and trigger players' minds—to get the best out of you. If you wanted to play football, you would pay close attention. There was a fear factor."

"Well, people tell you, and Andy Russell has written a couple of books, and even some of the old linemen—Jerry Wallach and Conrad Hitchler—who had been in the service thought of him as manipulative and looked at him with a little sarcasm when he would try some of his psychology," said Joe Buerkle, who lettered at Missouri from 1962 to 1964. "But after we played for him and graduated we thought he was a genius.... I remember him shouting at me personally one day, 'You should have run faster!' I was beating most of the people and he still wanted more."

Film review sessions after games could be brutal. Practice sessions after losses were even more demanding than the games.

"Yeah, you know even if you played a good game, he would get on you for something on Sunday," said Sam Adams, a linebacker, offensive guard-tackle, and co-captain of the 1969 team.

The fear factor was there, especially in the film sessions.

"If you showed signs of not getting job done, he would get rid of you," Reese said. "What he would do in the film sessions, he would turn off the projector. I have never seen another coach do this. He would reach over and turn it off and then yell and holler and it would be pitch dark in the room. He would say, 'Reese, Gus Otto'—it didn't matter who it was—'If you don't get it done, you won't be playing the position tomorrow.'"

Reese said if a player couldn't consistently execute on the "Missouri Sweep," the bread and butter of the Mizzou offense in the early 1960s, Devine would say, "You are never going to run the play again."

"He would not take away a scholarship," Reese said. "He would take the right to play away.… If you got a problem, you cut the snake's head off in front of everybody."

On the other hand, a player could be anointed during one of the practices.

"We are in two-a-days one year and it is war," said Tom Stephenson, a MU lineman in the late 1960s and early 1970s. "Devine is up in his tower drinking his milkshake and he says, 'George Fountain, you are a football player and you have a scholarship right now.' And he would say, 'Guys, is there anybody who doesn't think George should have a scholarship right now? Guys, go shake George's hand.' Seventy guys go shake his hand."

Devine's psychological ploys sometimes were even humorous or drew funny responses from players. Beating perennial Big Eight powers Oklahoma and Nebraska became a preoccupation with Devine.

Once, before the Tigers were playing Nebraska in the mid-1960s, Francis Peay opened his locker to find a cornhusk inside and wondered what it was. Trainer Fred Wappel had to tell Peay what it was. "You know we play Nebraska this week, and it's just a reminder about the big game from the coach," Wappel said.

"Damn good thing we ain't playing the Chicago Bears," Peay replied.

"During my senior year, we would come out of this small little training room, and there was a record player," Dennis Poppe, a defensive back, said of the 1969 season. "He played that thing all week, 'Boomer Sooner.' On Thursday, during our walk through, all of a sudden we hear the scraping sound of a needle on a record. We are joking around and it goes quiet. Devine is in the middle of the locker room and he said, 'I hope you are tired of the record!' And he tried breaking it over his knee, but he never did break it. He gives it a fling and it goes about 20 feet. We all are laughing so hard and trying to get out of the locker room because we didn't want him to see us laughing. He was a master motivational type of guy. We knew what he was trying to do."

And Missouri did beat Oklahoma and Heisman Trophy winner running back Steve Owens, 44–10, two days later. Devine obviously got his point across.

Reese said players were taught not to like Kansas, either.

"When you were freshmen at Missouri, you would go over to Harry Smith's house for hot dogs and hamburgers and there would be a Jayhawk hung up in a noose in the basement," Reese said.

Devine's Control Bred Cardinal Rules

Uniformity was a form of control at MU under Devine.

All the players wore black or gold blazers with ties on road trips, even when they stayed at a nearby Jefferson City, Missouri, hotel before home games, a practice Missouri would continue years after Devine left. There was a strict adherence to team rules—or else!—under Uncle Dan. No exceptions.

"Devine played with people's minds," Sam Adams said. "Ben Benhardt and I were together and we were going to play Oklahoma at OU. [Devine] was strict on all rules, what you could do and not do. [Ben and I] got candy out of the candy machine at the hotel and he brought it up at again at films on Sunday."

Beyond simple team rules were Devine's cardinal rules: don't make stupid mistakes in crucial situations, never lose to an inferior team, stand out in special team areas such as punting and kick returns (which often determine the outcome of games), and never let the other team's best player beat you.

"He was very much in control of everything," said John Burns, a MU lineman from 1967 to 1970. "He would come back to Missouri team reunions and semi-apologize for being tough on us. He would say, 'I didn't want you to jump offside when it was third and one.'"

"He was the most different coach I have ever been around, and I am sure he was a mystery to a lot of us," said MU end Russ Sloan of Devine. "What you have to recognize about him, what we did under him we did well.... We were very sound fundamentally, very well prepared, and didn't beat ourselves. He was a far, far different coach than Frank Broyles and Don Faurot."

During Devine's 13 seasons at Missouri, the Tigers were consistently excellent against the perceived bottom three teams in the Big Eight: Iowa State, Oklahoma State, and Kansas State. Missouri only lost one game to each of those teams during Devine's tenure.

"We never lost to Iowa State [until 1970, Devine's final season at Missouri]," said Stephenson. "If we had lost to Iowa State, what we would do on Sunday, Monday, and Tuesday, you couldn't imagine. He would be the meanest mother———."

Stephenson remembers one particularly brutal drill after a kick was returned for a touchdown in the previous game against Missouri in the late 1960s.

"When that punt was returned for a touchdown, it was the ugliest practice in Missouri history," Stephenson said. "They made a guy return a punt and made every guy hit him until he was down. All 11 people hit him and he broke his leg. Dan Devine never did that again."

Reese said that Devine would end practice with special team play—punting and punt returns during the final 15-20 minutes. "If you were on special teams and screwed it up, you were walking on the other side of street and away from the football players," Reese said.

One of the most remarkable stats of Missouri's defenses and Devine's persistence on stopping star players was the Tigers' work on Kansas's star running back, Gale Sayers. In three games against Missouri from 1962 to 1964, Sayers scored one touchdown on a five-yard run and the Jayhawks lost two of the contests (9–7 and 34–14) and tied the other (3–3).

In his senior year, Sayers carried the ball eight times for 19 yards. He never broke loose against the Tigers in any of the three games.

"Devine would not let the best player on your team beat him," Stephenson said. "Against Sayers, Devine would say, 'He is going to go off tackle, or around end and he is not going to cut it back inside…. If you have somebody else, bring that guy on, but Sayers doesn't beat us. Steve Owens [of Oklahoma] doesn't beat us; Jerry LeVias [of SMU] doesn't beat us. Go to those guys and they will tell you that [playing Missouri] was a miserable day for them."

And Heisman Trophy-winner Joe Bellino didn't beat Missouri, either. In the 1961 Orange Bowl, he was held to four yards rushing in a 21–14 Missouri victory.

"I was sure we could stop Bellino," Devine told the *St. Louis Globe-Democrat* after the game. "I have never been surer of anything in my life."

Eccentric to the Core

"He was an unusual guy, but because he was eccentric, he was a pretty darn good psychologist," said Missouri quarterback Phil Snowden of Devine.

Carl Reese, as a graduate assistant coach, remembers taking Devine to his television shows in St. Louis and Kansas City during one season in the mid-1960s. Devine was appearing on the show with Bob Broeg, sports editor of the *St. Louis Post-Dispatch*, on one of the shows and Reese was driving him to St.

Louis. Reese also had to help tape the show and put it together on the reel.

"I would go to the cleaners and pick up the clothes he was going to wear," Reese said. "And we were headed to St. Louis. He would be in the backseat and we would get to the outskirts of St. Louis and he would strip down and put on the clothes that I had picked up at the cleaners…. He was eccentric as far as cleanliness and looking sharp."

On one of those coach's shows in 1966, Devine also let some rare humor show through his eccentricities. After a 21–14 victory over Illinois in Champaign, Devine was co-hosting the Sunday night television show. During the first half of the show, the plays and the numbers of the uniforms were reversed because the film had been threaded the wrong way. When asked by the announcer if he made any halftime adjustments, Devine replied, "I told our passer to start passing right handed and our punter to kick with his right foot."

Once, conducting a postgame press conference in the cramped locker room, Devine got up on a chair. He answered all the reporters' questions before dressing, then dressed and was about to leave when he learned that another reporter had missed his postgame remarks and wondered if could he repeat them. So Devine took off his clothes, got up on the chair, and began his remarks to the lone reporter in an otherwise cleared-out locker room.

Current Oklahoma athletic director Joe Castiglione was in a coffee shop with Devine years later when Devine was athletic director at Missouri for a second time from 1992 to 1994 and Castiglione was his assistant. Devine was indeed a stickler for detail and consistency to the point of eccentricity.

He asked the waiter for some hot coffee. Castiglione said that Devine emphasized the word hot.

Soon the waiter was back with what he perceived as hot coffee. Devine took a couple of sips, then motioned the waiter back. "I really need some hot coffee," he told him.

Castiglione said this went on several times. The coffee would cool as Devine would talk, and Devine would keep the frustrated waiter busy trying to find hot coffee.

Expanding Recruiting, Improving Race Relations

Don Faurot basically wanted to close the borders of Missouri and recruit players from within the state. But Devine, like Broyles before him, wanted to expand those recruiting borders—and did. He ventured first into the Midwest, particularly in the Chicago area, central Illinois, Iowa, and the state of Michigan. Devine was from Minnesota and had been an assistant coach at Michigan State in the early 1950s under Biggie Munn and Duffy Daugherty before moving to Arizona State in 1955, so he knew those areas well.

Devine already knew that Texas was a fertile recruiting area because the Big Ten and western schools were tapping the area for African American athletes who were either leaving the state or going to historically black colleges such as Grambling State University, Texas Southern University, or Alcorn State University. The Texas-based Southwest Conference didn't have an African American football player until Jerry LeVias played for SMU in 1966, and the Southeastern Conference was lily-white in the 1960s.

"We kept a list," said Gil Brandt, the player personnel director for the Dallas Cowboys at the time. "I had a high school coach in the area who kept track of all the good [African American] players. And then schools like Wyoming and Michigan would come in and recruit them because they weren't going to Southwest Conference schools."

Devine started recruiting Texas with fervor. One of his early success stories was Corpus Christi's back Johnny Roland, who would later star for the St. Louis Cardinals in the National Football League. Roland opted for Missouri over Oklahoma and became an immediate impact player for the Tigers.

"Johnny Roland made a huge difference," Buerkle said. "He was a stellar athlete. He had a presence that spilled over to the rest of the guys. There was no jacking around when it came to football. He was somewhat unassuming and quiet. But he was lights-on and lights-out in drills or in the games."

In his first varsity game as a sophomore in 1962, Roland made his presence felt in a 21–10 season-opening victory at California. Roland factored in all three Mizzou touchdowns that day. He carried the ball 20 times for 171 yards, a whopping 8.5 yards-a-carry average. His 58-yard touchdown run midway through the third quarter put the game out of reach. Roland even caught a touchdown pass.

"Roland was special," said Reese, who was one of the Missouri tri-captains with Roland in 1965. "He knew it, we knew it, and the coaches knew it…. He didn't have great speed, but he had the best balance of anybody I saw at that time."

Roland led Missouri in rushing for only his sophomore season, when he averaged 5.2 yards a carry. He was suspended by Devine for the 1963 season for allegedly taking wheels and tires from another student's car and putting them on his car. But he came back for the 1964 and 1965 seasons.

"Once he took a fall for things that were not his doing, he came back and played defense," Bill Tobin said. "He later was drafted by the Cardinals in the fourth round and played offense for the Cardinals. He was thin, long, and mean. He was *Esquire*-esque as far as dressing. He could style. He always looked very neat and very trim. We called him 'Pants.'… He was long and lean and muscular. He had what we called 'cable strength.'"

Roland made All-Big Eight in each of the years he played and was an All-American as a senior on the Tigers' Sugar Bowl team. He was part of a long list of African American athletes to come out of the Lone Star State and play for Missouri.

"I know we did not have the first black player in the conference because Oklahoma did [with Prentiss Gautt in 1957]," said Tom Stephenson. "But where did Prentiss Gautt wind up? At the University of Missouri as an assistant coach…. [Devine] was the

Halfback Johnny Roland streaks to a 35-yard gain during Missouri's 21–10 season-opening victory over Cal in 1962. Roland, who later starred in the NFL, was Missouri's first African American team captain.

most color-blind person I had ever seen. If you asked him about 40 people on a roster, and say 'white-black-white-black,' I think he would get three or four wrong."

While Broyles had broken the color barrier in football at MU, Devine took race relations to new heights with his recruiting and organization. He had African Americans as co-captains or tri-captains (Johnny Roland in 1965, Jon Staggers in 1969, and Joe Moore in 1970), integrated the cheerleading squad, allowed players to select the cheerleaders, and started pairing African American players and white players as roommates.

Columbia, Missouri, was not exactly most the liberal place in America when it came to race relations. Missouri was a border state during the Civil War, and the Columbia area was known as

"Little Dixie." At one time, Confederate flags were flown at Missouri home football games and there was a Confederate soldier war memorial on campus. The bitter rivalry with free-state Kansas went all the way back to the Civil War.

But Devine was changing the culture around the football team, at least.

"He wanted to diversify the team," said Dennis Poppe. "Jon Staggers and I were roommates. He made sure a white guy and black guy would room together. He did things like that to teach you more than winning and losing."

Missouri had several African American players on its squad when it traveled to Little Rock for a game against Coach Frank Broyles' Arkansas team in 1963. It was a heated contest in which Missouri won on an extra point, 7–6. Reese remembers the aftermath more than he does the game. Playing in the South was not easy for an integrated college team in the 1960s.

"That was a game where we would eat a meal somewhere, they would not feed the black players, and we left," Reese remembers. "I know Devine would not have his black players eat in another room. I think that might have fired up the team.

"After the game, we saw our buses with the big 'N' word on it," Reese continued. "It had been spray painted on the bus. We had won the football game and we tried to leave. They were shaking the buses. I had a fear for my life."

The Tobin Brothers

Bill Tobin was a four-sport star at Maryville High School in Maryville, Missouri, in the late 1950s. He was recruited to Missouri by assistant coach Clay Cooper. He would become an important cog in Missouri football as a halfback-linebacker-kicker from 1960 to 1962.

In the Tigers' 10–7 victory over Kansas in 1961, Bill Tobin accounted for all of the Tigers' points by kicking the extra point and a field goal, and running for a score. To show his versatility, Tobin

Vince Tobin (41) completes a touchdown pass to Johnny Roland (23) in the Tigers' 21–10 victory over the California Bears in Berkeley, on September 22, 1962.

almost sarcastically points out he was the Tigers' leading pass receiver as a senior in 1962, with three catches in 10 regular-season games. As a two-way player who could also play special teams, Tobin was made for the limited substitution rules of that era.

But his little brother, Vince, was not nearly as heavily recruited.

"Vince was two years younger," Bill Tobin recalls. "His senior year [in high school] he tears up his knee and Vince doesn't play a lot. And he wasn't getting recruited. I went into talk to Clay Cooper. And Clay asks, 'Is he any good?' I hesitated a moment and said, 'He's my brother.' They gave him a partial scholarship."

That partial scholarship wouldn't last long. "Kansas had Gale Sayers on the freshman team and he tried to run outside three times," Bill Tobin said. "Vince Tobin tackled him all three times for no gain. At the end of game, Dan Devine came down from the stands and said, 'You are on [full] scholarship. Vince went on to play as a defensive back."

The next three years, with Vince Tobin on the Missouri defense, Gale Sayers never did break loose when playing against the Tigers. Vince Tobin also threw a touchdown pass on his very first play on the varsity.

"We went to Cal his sophomore year, which was my senior year," Bill Tobin recalls. "Vince comes in. Johnny Roland is the right halfback and he's the left back. Vince comes in for me and throws a left-handed pass to Johnny Roland for a touchdown. We were challenging the corners. He was on sweep and pulls up and throws it. That's what we would do—we would run and run the ball down their throats. And then when they got too aggressive [on defense] we would throw it over the top."

In 1962, Bill Tobin's best play was one of his last plays in the 14–10 victory over Georgia Tech in the Bluebonnet Bowl in Houston. Tobin took off on a 77-yard run against Georgia Tech for a touchdown. He broke over left tackle, cut back to the middle, got a key block from Andy Russell, and headed for the goal line. Don Toner of Georgia Tech made a dive for him at the nine, but to no avail.

"We were not supposed to be able to hold up against Georgia Tech," Tobin said. "It was a tooth-and-nail game. It was a very tight ballgame. We had a lot of tight games. That's the way football was played then—defense, special teams, and a lot of field position. We were backed up and played the counter reverse. Roland was the wingback and Russell was the fullback. I was able to break through a tackle. And nobody was fast enough to catch me."

"That game was all about the Bill Tobins and a few defensive players putting in a hell of day," Buerkle said. "Carl Crawford, a defensive back, intercepted it or broke up a pass. And this kid, his vertical leap was twice whatever it had been. It typified for me that everybody was playing over their heads."

Missouri's Aggressive Defense

From 1960 to 1962, the Tigers had an All-American at end or tackle, with Danny LaRose (end) in 1960, Ed Blaine (tackle) in 1961, and Conrad Hitchler (end) in 1962, each accomplishing the feat as a senior. LaRose and Hitchler were rush ends who pressured the passer.

"When it came to defense, it was Al Onofrio's game," said Buerkle, who played linebacker on defense. "He was a defensive mastermind. Yes, our ends were quite unique. Our defense was ahead of the game. It would not work too well today. It is just a different game."

Missouri's 1960 Big Eight title team didn't give up more than eight points in a contest until Oklahoma scored 19 in week 9 and

Missouri's defense, shown here harassing the quarterback from all sides in the 1961 Orange Bowl against Navy, may have been the top defense in the nation from 1960–1962.

Kansas scored 23 points in the Jayhawks' forfeited victory, the 10th game of the season. The Tigers' 1961 team allowed only 57 points, the fewest since the 1941 Missouri Sugar Bowl team controlled the ball and allowed only 39 points. And in 1962, Missouri ranked fifth nationally in total defense (181.1 yards a game) and fifth in scoring defense (5.2 points a game).

Buerkle remembers his fondest moment as a defender in the 1963 season opener against Northwestern. A couple of plays exemplified Mizzou's rush defense during the season-opening 23–12 loss to the Wildcats.

"Tommy Myers was their quarterback and had been on the front of Street & Smith's," Buerkle recalled. "Myers was picking us apart. And I have film of this game. They were moving toward the north goal line. And Coach Onofrio turned me loose to go after Myers. I put him on his back twice and he lost yardage twice. The third time, he didn't let me blitz. And Myers dropped back. We had a punter who was not so fast on foot playing defensive back. We were short of defensive backs. And he couldn't cover the back in a short yardage situation. It turned the game. But I relished getting off the top of Tommy Myers."

Lane Takes Over as Quarterback

In 1963, Gary Lane became the Tigers' signal-caller for three seasons and led the Tigers in passing and scoring those years and even in rushing as a junior in 1964. From 1960 to 1962, with Ron Taylor and Jim Johnson as the main quarterbacks, the Tigers were groundhogs, especially in 1962 when they completed just 24 passes as a team. And Missouri didn't complete a pass against Georgia Tech in the Bluebonnet Bowl.

Things loosened up in 1963, in more ways than one. Lane was a character from East Alton, Illinois, and didn't mix as well with many of Missouri's home-grown players.

"If he hadn't been the kind of personality he was, he would have been better appreciated," Buerkle said. "He had an ego problem.... This was a Missouri team through and through and he looked a little bit different. He wasn't as smooth. He had a 1957 black Chevy and he had a tachometer [on the dashboard]. His nickname became 'Tach.' He was a very good athlete. I thought Mike Jones from Kennett, Missouri, was a better pure quarterback. But he didn't have the same speed. Gary was more of a roll-out, throw-on-the-run type player. He was truly a character."

"Gary Lane was an exceptional athlete," Carl Reese said. "At that time, we were running a little option off play action. He had speed and quickness. He later was an NFL official. He was mobile. He would take off and go."

During each of Lane's seasons, however, the Tigers started off with losses: to Northwestern in 1963, to California in 1964, and to Kentucky in 1965. And Nebraska, under Bob Devaney, began a run of four straight Big Eight championships from 1963 to 1966, corresponding to a four-game winning streak over Missouri.

In 1963, Missouri finished lower than second in the league—for the first time under Devine's leadership—when it ended up third behind Nebraska and Oklahoma. In 1964, the Tigers were fourth behind Nebraska, Oklahoma and Kansas.

The four straight losses to Nebraska, in particular, ignited a heated rivalry between Devaney and Devine, two Irishmen who had both served as assistant coaches on the Michigan State staff in the early 1950s.

Lane always brought Missouri within striking distance of beating Nebraska, but he never could win. The most contentious was the 1965 16–14 loss to the Huskers in Columbia decided by a fourth-quarter 26-yard field goal by Nebraska's Larry Wachholtz. A controversial personal foul penalty was called on Missouri senior Bruce Van Dyke to put the kicker in position to win the game.

Francis Peay's Change of Sides

Missouri's big tackle Francis Peay—a Pittsburgh, Pennsylvania, native—was recruited out of Oklahoma's Cameron State Agricultural College (now Cameron University) as a defensive tackle. Rollie Dotsch, the Tigers' offensive line coach at the time, discovered that Peay needed to be on his side of the ball early in the 1964 season.

"They recruited him as a defensive tackle, and as good and big and strong as he was, he didn't have the natural movement and he couldn't play defensive tackle," Reese said. "The coaches had spent a lot of time recruiting him. And they were mad. He wasn't good enough to start. But he was a specimen.

"Rollie ended up saying, 'You guys don't think he can play. Let me have him.' Francis wasn't showing much. And we had lost to Cal. Rollie said, 'I will take him.' Rollie goes out there with Peay and

Offensive tackle Francis Peay was named AP's Lineman of the Week in November 1965 as the Tigers gained 295 yards rushing against Oklahoma in a 30–0 win.

there were 80, 90 guys, either true freshmen or red-shirt freshmen. He got Francis Peay one-on-one out there one day with
some of these guys. They were knocking him back and he was
sending bodies flying. Francis was taking all these licks...and
Rollie sent him out the next day and then for four or five days. This
guy, something happened to him. Rollie started training him. Not
long after that he started at tackle and he was like a big spider. He
came off the football and was a great offensive tackle."

Peay became an All-American tackle in 1965 as a Mizzou
senior and played nine seasons in the NFL with three different
teams, the New York Giants, Green Bay Packers, and Kansas City
Chiefs.

"He was a very athletic tackle," said Gil Brandt, player personnel director for the Dallas Cowboys at the time." He was probably
the highest-paid football player at the time. He came out and
signed with the Giants and it was the last of the war [between the
NFL and the AFL]."

Getting Some Sugar

Missouri started the 1965 season on a horrendous note, suffering
seven turnovers (four lost fumbles and three interceptions) in a
7–0 loss to Kentucky in Columbia. It was perhaps the most error-
filled game during the Devine years. But Missouri would lose only
one more game the entire season on the way to an 8–2–1 record
and a No. 6 final national ranking.

Missouri rebounded after the Kentucky disaster to shut out
Oklahoma State, 13–0, and beat Minnesota, 17–6. Both games
were on the road. Against the Golden Gophers, Lane accounted
for both touchdowns in Mizzou's ball-control offense. One of
Lane's touchdowns was on a great run behind a crunching block
by Francis Peay.

The Tigers operated from a Wing-T formation, utilizing a balanced and unbalanced line with a split end. The basic plays were
a sweep, an off-tackle power belly, and option series with counters

and dives. The Tigers finished third nationally rushing with 247.3 yards a game. Missouri went to a six-man line, with two linebackers and three-deep secondary and allowed only 8.3 points a game during the regular season.

Besides the losses to Kentucky and Nebraska, the only other blemish on the Tigers' 1965 season was a 14–14 tie against UCLA in Columbia.

Missouri trailed the Bruins and quarterback Gary Beban, 14–0, going into the fourth quarter. But two Tigers special team plays helped tie the score when Ray Thorpe ran a kickoff back 79 yards for a touchdown and Johnny Roland returned a punt 65 yards for another score. Lane failed on a conversion pass after the first touchdown, but then passed to Earl Denny for the two tying points on a conversion pass after the second touchdown. UCLA went on to beat Michigan State in the Rose Bowl that season.

Despite the loss to Nebraska, which cost Mizzou the Big Eight title, the Tigers won the rest of their league games. They beat Oklahoma, 30–0, and accepted a bid to play in the Sugar Bowl. Missouri had not beaten Oklahoma in Columbia since 1945 and had not shut out the Sooners since 1941. But the 1965 Tigers piled up 295 rushing yards on the Sooners, with Lane running for three touchdowns, passing for another, and accounting for 155 yards of total offense.

Missouri players were not told of the bid, which was contingent upon them beating OU, until after they had won. And the Sugar opponent was Florida with quarterback Steve Spurrier, who would win the Heisman Trophy a year later and had already developed quite a reputation as a junior.

"The whole time we were told he could do this and he could do that," Reese said. "We get to the game and we jumped ahead. Then the momentum changed. They went for two points [after touchdowns] three times and didn't make a one. But if Spurrier had had another drive and the game had gone longer, they would have beaten us. I remember the game early being kind of fun."

Florida trailed 20–0 going into fourth quarter. Then, Spurrier completed 16 passes in the final 15 minutes alone and took the Gators on scoring drives of 89, 81, and 10 yards, the latter after the Gators recovered a Tiger fumble. Spurrier became the first player on a losing team to be named the Most Outstanding Player of the Sugar Bowl. He set five Sugar Bowl records at the time, completing 27 of 45 passes for 352 yards at Tulane Stadium.

Turning Down Bowl Bids

In the 1960s, there were far fewer bowls and there was less demand for football to support low-revenue college sports. At Missouri, players voted on bowl invitations. Athletic budgets weren't part of the controlling equation.

The Big Eight normally sent a team to the Orange Bowl, its champion. Players understood that. But other offers would come up for a vote.

"It was amazing how times have changed," said Dennis Poppe, a MU defensive back in the late 1960s. "They would say, 'You guys vote on it.'"

In 1963, as an example, the Tigers we were 7–3 and ranked 16th in the United Press International poll, coming off a 9–7 victory over Kansas.

"Some seniors on the football team had had enough and had worked hard," said Reese, who was a sophomore at the time. "We had won the game and were given a chance to go to a bowl. Coach Devine said, 'I am going to leave it to a vote of the seniors.' They voted it down. He said, 'Okay, let the team vote, seniors notwithstanding.' One of the seniors kicks me in the butt and gives me a dirty look. The team voted not to go to bowl."

"We had already missed Thanksgiving," Buerkle said, alluding to the fact the KU game had been postponed because of President Kennedy's assassination. "And most of us had gone to the Bluebonnet Bowl the year before. We didn't want to spend Christmas at a secondary bowl."

Johnny Roland (23) turns the corner in the 14–10 MU win against Georgia Tech in the 1962 Bluebonnet Bowl. Missouri was a regular bowl participant during the 1960s, and even turned down bids to "secondary" bowls three times during the decade.

In 1964, despite a 6–3–1 record, a 34–14 season-ending victory over Kansas, and a No. 18 ranking by United Press International, the Tiger seniors said "no thanks" to a postseason bid. After the 1967 season, the Tigers also turned down a bid to the Liberty Bowl despite a 7–3 record.

"We voted down the Liberty Bowl my sophomore year," Sam Adams said. "Back then, there were only eight or nine bowls. I think it was more influence of the coaches. I don't think Dan Devine wanted to play in the Liberty Bowl."

chapter 5
Gator, Orange Letdown

"I was able to mature as a football player and as a man under that program with the help from a coaching staff that was second to none."

—Roger Wehrli

A New Quarterback in Columbia

Missouri's offense was producing rather modest statistics under quarterback Gary Kombrink during the 1966 and 1967 seasons. Missouri averaged only 12.1 points a game in 1966 and 13.4 points in 1967 as the Tigers posted solid seasons (6–3–1 and 7–3) with their unrelenting defense, good kicking game, and modest offense.

But there was a need for Coach Dan Devine to go out and recruit a top-notch quarterback to get the Tigers back in contention for the Big Eight title.

Devine was out scouring the recruiting trails for that key player. His travels took him to Osawatomie, Kansas, and the home of future NFL quarterback Lynn Dickey.

"When he [Devine] recruited me, I committed to Missouri two weeks prior to the signing date," Dickey said. "I remember him saying, 'Thank you.' But before he could get to the curb, I remember my dad said to me, 'I think that was a bad decision. He's had a lot of guys go there through the years and they never have thrown it more than 20 times a game. Why do you think he is going to change it for a guy from Osawatomie, Kansas?'

"I started thinking he might be right," Dickey continued. "Vince Gibson said he was going to throw it 40 times a game and run a pro-style offense. And Kansas State was building a new stadium. But I didn't know they hadn't won a game [since the 1964 season]. What kid with ESPN these days wouldn't know that? I think I was a little green."

So, Dickey reconsidered his choice and eventually signed with the Wildcats and played for Gibson, the "Purple People Eaters," and later the Houston Oilers and Green Bay Packers.

"Keith Weber, whose brother Chuck Weber was a receiver at Missouri, worked in the athletic department. I tried to get ahold of him and tell him [I had changed my mind]," Dickey continued. "I finally got ahold of somebody there and they said he was on his way to Kansas. He comes all the way out there, and I told him I was really sorry and I had tried to get ahold of him, but I had changed my mind.

After Devine recruited Terry McMillan from Florida, the two would develop a winning rapport that led to a dynamic Tiger offense.

"I don't think [Devine] lost any sleep over it," Dickey said of his change of heart. "Terry McMillan was the perfect guy. He came from a junior college and was an option guy."

Devine recruited Floridian McMillan out of what is now Missouri Southern State University in Joplin, Missouri. And McMillan, eligible for the 1968 season, could throw the ball well, if he was allowed to in the offense, although that would become much more apparent in 1969 when he would pass for nearly 2,000 yards.

"McMillan coming in settled our team," said Dennis Poppe, an MU defensive back. "He fit in real quick. He had an outgoing personality. He had charisma. He was a gunslinger who was not afraid to throw the ball. He had a good arm. He was a good teammate. He was confident. He had an air about him good quarterbacks have. You knew he was pretty sure of himself. His confidence spilled over to his teammates.

"We had an athletic dorm and before spring practice or the season, in one of the fields next to the dorm where we lived, we were doing a little one-on-one, running pass patterns," Poppe continued. "He was throwing it. And I could tell he had an arm. He would tell me, 'For a big boy, you close pretty fast.' He was encouraging. I would lay off and close and knock the ball away. He had come from being not even starting at quarterback in high school. But he knew what it took."

Missouri's offensive numbers went up dramatically in 1968 and 1969, in part because of McMillan and also because of several other new skilled players on offense: nimble halfback Joe Moore, bruising fullback James Harrison, all-purpose runner Jon Staggers, and swift wide receiver Mel Gray.

This blended with Missouri's solid line play, defensive commitment, and excellent special teams play to vault the Tigers back into Big Eight title contention and, in 1969, give them a shot at the national title.

Missouri's Pro Quad Formula:
Moore, Harrison, Gray, Staggers

From a skill standpoint, this was undoubtedly the golden era of Missouri football. Moore, Harrison, Gray, and Staggers would all go on to play in the NFL with varying success. But they were all excellent college players, all putting on some dazzling exhibitions at Mizzou during their careers.

"Joe Moore was my age and he was just a physical specimen," said John Burns, a Missouri offensive lineman. "My understanding [was] his main accomplishments in high school were more as a nose guard. He was certainly very quick and strong. It was kind of unusual. He and Harrison were both draft picks by the Chicago Bears. Joe got too active in the union and was blackballed by the NFL. But he was a good guy. [Running back] Ron McBride was one of hardest-nosed players I have been around. Those guys were tough, competitive guys, and real good in the type of offense we ran."

Tom Stephenson, another MU player during that era, remembers what Moore brought to the team. And it was much more than just physical ability, which allowed him to rush for just more than 1,300 yards in 1969.

"You didn't have to run your mouth to be a leader," Stephenson said. "You could say a few words. Joe Moore was a hero to me. Every day or two, he would say, 'Pick it up. Pick it up.' Classic

Bruising Missouri halfback Joe Moore drags a Penn State player for extra yards in the 1970 Orange Bowl.

example: You are a halfback and you get the ball on a handoff on a dummy play, not against a defensive line, how far you do run? You run the ball five yards and then you run back. How far did Joe Moore run, 20 yards? That means he has to run back 20 yards, catch his breath, and run the next play. Why do that? He was showing us that is how you do it. Denny Poppe was the same way. He would put the wood to your ass.

"Joe Moore was the greatest player at Missouri to ever have the ball under his arms," Stephenson added. "If you needed 3½ yards, he got 3½ yards. Who else did that? Every single time, he did it. He didn't have the great stats some other guys had. But we didn't feed him the ball that much. Understand James Harrison was 6'4½", weighed 235 pounds, had a 34 inch waist, and ran 40 in 4.4 when the pros came down and timed Mel Gray. It made Terry McMillan's life easier throwing to him. When the pros timed James Harrison, he tied Mel Gray in the 40-yard dash. I was there. I saw it. And Harrison was taken as the second pick in the second round by the Bears."

Harrison was part of Devine's Texas connection, coming from San Antonio. Moore was from Beaumont High School in St. Louis and Staggers, who actually led Missouri in receiving yards in 1968, was from Jefferson City, Missouri. Californian Gray, a sprinter, was a junior college star out of Fort Scott Community College in Kansas.

"We were going through practice, and it was a point of pride with the defensive backs," Poppe said. "I thought we would introduce [Gray] to the Big Eight. The first time we went one-on-one, he wasn't paying attention. I hit him with a forearm and bumped him around. The next time I took a swing at him and all I hit was air. He was outstanding, real compact and well proportioned."

And he provided Missouri with a dimension of speed for the long pass that they eventually would exploit. Gray averaged 22.2 yards a catch as a Tiger. In the NFL, he was also a big-play threat with the old St. Louis Football Cardinals.

"Mel Gray was a great kickoff and return guy and a great wide receiver," the Dallas Cowboys' Gil Brandt said. "He was a great speed guy and used to wreak havoc on us. It seems to me in 1975, he had a big year and he had 11 touchdown passes. Any time he played us, he had a career game."

Mizzou's Forearm Shiver

Missouri's defensive toughness under Devine and his architect Al Onofrio was legendary throughout the Big Eight Conference. Years later, opposing players still talked about the blows they would receive from some of the Tigers, who might have been light of body but heavy on moxie.

"We had a conference room at the Orange Bowl, and we would have receptions there and tell old jokes," remembers Steve Hatchell, former executive director of the Orange Bowl from 1987 to 1993 and now executive director of the National Football Foundation. "It was when we had our Orange Bowl offices at the stadium. And I always remember we would have guys from Oklahoma, Kansas, and other schools from the Big Eight and they would tell you what it was like to play Missouri in the late 1960s and early 1970s under Devine and Onofrio. Missouri played this defensive style where they would squat and use a one-arm shiver. One of their players was Rocky Wallace, who was on the defensive line and wore glasses.

"When you played games at Missouri, even the Oklahoma and Nebraska guys would say you might win, but they were painful to play. They would beat you to death. When Missouri played you, they would bludgeon you. The great OU teams might win there 10–7 or 6–3.

"I remember one of the guys at one of the receptions," Hatchell continued. "His name was Byron Bigby. He played at Oklahoma and got into a game against Missouri when another couple of players got hurt. He said. 'I think I am the greatest OU lineman. I am going to change the way they play offense. I get into the game, and Rocky Wallace is staring at me and he puts up his forearm and hits it three times, like I am going to get you. I went from being the best lineman to being petrified. Rocky Wallace hit me and I had a tingling up and down my spine.'"

Poppe said the Missouri defensive linemen were taught the technique.

"We would give a forearm to an opponent to see which way he was trying to block you," Poppe said. "You would give the forearm and jump where you thought he wanted to be."

And the Tigers had to be tough because of their lack of size compared to frequently bigger opponents on either side of the ball.

"Devine never got into weight lifting," said John Burns, an MU offensive lineman under Devine. "We almost always were undersized. With the offense Missouri played, we could get away with it."

Wehrli: A Star is Born

In its history, Missouri has only two Pro Football Hall of Fame players—defensive back Roger Wehrli (1966–68 at MU) and tight end Kellen Winslow (1976–78 at MU). They played a decade apart, on different sides of the ball, and were from completely different backgrounds. But they had one thing in common. Neither player had a tremendous buildup before he arrived in Columbia.

Wehrli was from the tiny western Missouri town of King City, and was actually a better basketball player than a football player in high school. Winslow had hardly played high school basketball and had a city background, having grown up in East St. Louis, Illinois. But both were All-Americans by the time they left MU and went on to great pro careers.

"I never thought my football career would be that long,'" Wehrli said when he was inducted into the Pro Football Hall of Fame in August of 2007. "I kind of expected to play basketball in college. In fact, I remember taking off those pads the last game my senior year [of high school] and throwing them down and said, 'That is the last time I will put those things on.' I couldn't have been more wrong.

Defensive back Roger Wehrli, who played for the Tigers from 1966 to 1968, is one of only two Missouri alumni in the Pro Football Hall of Fame.

"I received some offers from some small colleges to play basketball. But it was my successes at the state track meet my senior year that caught the eye of the Missouri football coaches, who thought I might have the speed and quickness to play football at Mizzou. So out of the blue I was offered a scholarship to the University of Missouri and I took it even though I wondered if I had what it took to play major college football.... I was able to mature as a football player and as a man under that program with the help from a coaching staff that was second to none. Coach [Clay] Cooper was basically the man who taught me how to play defensive back."

Wehrli intercepted 10 passes during his career at Missouri, with seven coming during his senior season in 1968, when he also led the nation in punt returns. Poppe, a converted quarterback who played in the same defensive backfield as a safety, was hurt midway through the 1968 season in the Tigers' 16–14 victory over Nebraska in Lincoln. That injury gave rise to Wehrli's stardom.

"I got my arm broken in the Nebraska game and I tell [Wehrli] I made him an All-American when they switched him to safety," Poppe said. "He took my position after that game. Talk about a tough game… I suffered the broken arm, a jammed back, and hit jaw. I could hardly swallow. I had to stand up on the airplane coming home.

"But Roger was a great athlete, with so much speed former safety [Poppe] didn't have. He covered a lot of ground, And they couldn't throw away from him in the middle of the field."

Wehrli was truly a scoring weapon on special teams because he often—particularly in victories over Iowa State and Army during the 1968 season—gave the Tigers great field position to score with his punt and kickoff returns.

Sam Adams remembers Wehrli having a light moment during the 1968 Kansas State game: "He could hit you and hurt you. We were setting up a punt return and we were forming a line to the right. But Roger was pointing to the left. The punter was running toward him and passing us up. He made the tackle."

Wehrli went on to an outstanding career with the old St. Louis Football Cardinals, playing his entire career there (14 seasons) and being named All-NFL five times. He had 40 career interceptions and returned punts the first seven seasons of his professional career

"I think he was the last Caucasian corner to play in the league," the Cowboys' Gil Brandt said. "He had unusual speed."

That Gator Bowl Season

Missouri started out the 1968 season with a 12–6 loss at Kentucky, but then they won seven straight games. After the loss to the Wildcats, the following Saturday the Tigers shut out Illinois in Champaign, 44–0, which was Missouri's most lopsided non-conference road victory during the Devine era.

It also emphasized the dominance Devine's Missouri teams showed against Big Ten Conference teams: they were 10–1–1 during his 13-year Tigers coaching career.

With Wehrli, Rocky Wallace, and company, Missouri statistically was the best defense in the Big Eight in 1968, ranking first in rushing defense, passing defense, total defense, and scoring defense. Wehrli's seven interceptions led the league.

"They have to be the toughest team we have played," Kansas's John Zook said at the end of the regular season. "They are probably the hardest-hitting team we have played. And their backs have better speed as a whole than any team we played."

Despite the presence of McMillan, the Tigers were hugging the ground with their stable of good running backs. In fact, on October 12, 1968, Missouri set a record for NCAA rushing attempts in a game with 99 in a 27–14 victory over Colorado in which the Tigers rushed for 421 yards. That record still stands today.

With a 7–1 record, 5–0 in the Big Eight, sixth-ranked Missouri went to play old nemesis Oklahoma in Norman and lost, 28–14. That dropped Missouri to the Gator Bowl. Kansas was slated to go to the Orange Bowl, despite the fact that Missouri could still gain a share of the Big Eight title with a victory over the Jayhawks. Kansas—intercepting a McMillan pass for a touchdown—and KU quarterback Bobby Douglass, looking sharp, jumped out to a quick 14–0 lead.

Trailing early against the Jayhawks, Devine allowed McMillan to put the ball in the air, and he completed 16 of 24 passes for 233 yards. He showed glimpses of what was in store for Tigers fans in 1969. But Missouri fell just short, 21–19, against Kansas.

"I don't think we could have asked for any more effort," Devine said after the game. "I am sure there were a lot of people who were apprehensive about us getting run out of the stadium when it was 14–0, and it took a great effort not to get run out.... Kansas will make a great representative in the Orange Bowl for the Big Eight. They were difficult to move the ball against and were difficult to defend. They just have a well-rounded team."

With a 7–3 record and coming off two straight losses, respect for the Tigers was not that great in Jacksonville, Florida.

"Bear Bryant was the king down there," Poppe said. "I don't think they thought of Missouri as a worthy opponent. That's the

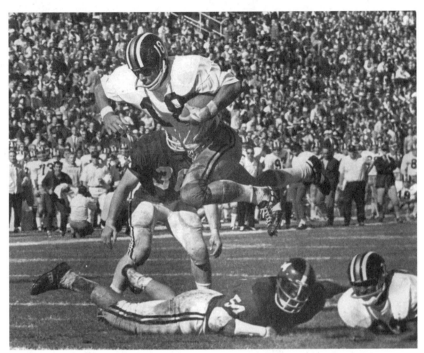

Missouri quarterback Terry McMillan leaps over an Alabama defender and scores from the 4-yard line in the 1968 Gator Bowl, a 35–10 Tiger victory.

media and fans. Before the game, we stayed at an Air Force base. And on the pillows, on the bed, it said 'Roll Tide.' At least mine did. I thought, Man we are in 'Bama territory! At the pregame luncheon, Bear [Bryant] gets up and gets a standing ovation."

Despite the obvious Jacksonville bias toward Alabama, McMillan scored three times against Alabama in the Gator Bowl, all on runs, and became the first Tiger to score three touchdowns in a bowl game. The Tigers didn't complete a pass against the Crimson Tide, although they had two intercepted. Missouri gained all 402 of its yards on the ground on 82 rushing attempts, still a Gator Bowl record for carries.

Meanwhile, Missouri's defense held Alabama to a still–Gator Bowl record minus 45 yards rushing and only 32 yards of total offense. Poppe intercepted a pass and returned it 47 yards for a touchdown as the Tigers used a 21-point fourth quarter to blow out the Tide.

Devine, despite his rather brusque exterior, could be a softie sometimes, as exhibited in his letter to a player's mother that season before the Gator Bowl.

"My dad died on October 30 of that year," Tom Stephenson said. "Everybody thought Devine was a hard ass. And he was. But he was an Irish hard ass. And he had a heart that melted from time to time. I get selected to go to the Gator Bowl, one of the redshirt freshmen to go down. He wrote my mother a letter: 'We are going to be down there during Christmas, your son's first Christmas away since his dad died, who we all miss. It would be nice if there was something underneath the tree for him.' So she sent him a gift to put under the tree in Jacksonville."

On a much lighter note, these Tigers in the late 1960s could have some fun with their coaches.

"It was either my junior or sophomore year," said Sam Adams. "John Kadlec had come back [after serving as an assistant coach at Kansas State]. One of the older guys had a chocolate cake sent to the coaches full of ex-lax. Al Onofrio, Kadlec, and Hank Kuhlmann started eating the cake. Halfway through practice, Kadlec couldn't make it to the bathroom and messed in his britches."

Orange Bowl Season of 1969

Entering the 1969 season, the Tigers had had trouble getting started in four of the previous six seasons, when they lost openers. And it appeared they were going to lose their fifth opener in seven years as Air Force struck for a touchdown in the final minute on a long pass. McMillan countered with a long pass of his own to John Henley for a 66-yard gain to the Air Force 24.

A couple of running plays to the 14, sandwiched around time-outs, allowed Henry Brown to kick a field goal in the closing seconds for a titillating 19–17 season-opening Missouri win.

"I think that game made it that year for us," Tom Stephenson said. "We had played poorly. Air Force played with great enthusiasm. They were a well-coached, aggressive team. And that was the only thing that could beat us. We were well-coached, aggressive, and we weren't big. And we were like playing in a mirror all day. We played some very ordinary football against them. But in the end, we kicked a field goal with time running out. And that made us think we were special."

In the next game, Missouri roughed up Illinois, 37–6, in St. Louis, the first of three games over two seasons to be played at Busch Memorial Stadium, the home of the St. Louis Baseball and Football Cardinals. Joe Moore had a big day, with 185 yards rushing. Missouri's speed on offense was even more of a factor on the AstroTurf, although that same carpet was showing signs of trouble that the following season would plague the Tigers against Air Force. Missouri defenders' feet were getting caught in it doing drills.

Certainly, ninth-ranked Missouri's trip to Ann Arbor the following week would demonstrate where their season was going. The Tigers handed Bo Schembechler his first loss as Michigan's coach, as they had done to Bump Elliott, Schembechler's predecessor, in Ann Arbor in 1959.

The Tigers jumped to a 24–3 lead, then held off the Wolverines by scoring 16 points in the fourth quarter for a 40–17 victory over a Michigan team that would go to the Rose Bowl.

Poppe intercepted a pass and got the game ball because of the birth of his son, John Henry Poppe. The game ball disappeared years ago, as John Henry played catch with it and took it to school for show and tell. But Poppe can still remember the Mizzou defense that season, which was light on its feet against bigger opponents, such as Michigan's offensive line that featured Dan Dierdorf.

"Our defense was real quick and small and had pretty good unity," Poppe said. "And it was a little bit unorthodox, the wide tackle six."

Missouri returned to Columbia and won its first two Big Eight games against Nebraska, 17–7, and Oklahoma State,

31–21, before traveling to Boulder, Colorado, to face a talented, yet inconsistent Colorado team that would finish 8–3. The Buffalos defeated fifth-ranked Missouri, 31–24, on a field that was hard to play on because sand had been laid down on it to absorb the mud and wetness brought on by inclement, snowy weather.

"It wasn't the mud so much," Stephenson said. "They had some players. Colorado coach Eddie Crowder had a team that played pretty well one weekend, then didn't play well. It was not like they were a bunch of nobodies."

Later, Colorado finished third in the Big Eight behind co-champions Missouri and Nebraska and handed Alabama a 47–33 loss in the Liberty Bowl.

Missouri had little time to recover from the defeat in Boulder because improved Kansas State was coming to town with junior quarterback Lynn Dickey, who had directed the Wildcats to an astonishing 59–21 victory over Oklahoma in Manhattan, the Wildcats' first over the Sooners since 1934. Kansas State was ranked 12th with a 5–1 record.

"It was probably the first game I ever played in when I was in the huddle, I wished I was in the stands watching it," Dickey said of the Missouri game. "It was back and forth, back and forth. We knew we would be in for a tough game and we didn't play well in the first half. I remember going in, I was dreading facing [Wildcats head coach] Vince Gibson at halftime. When things weren't going well, he didn't take it well."

Dickey remembers Gibson didn't say much to the team at halftime. The Wildcats were facing a 21–6 deficit, which probably served as a great motivating force to the Wildcats during the final 30 minutes.

"I didn't see it at the time," Dickey said. "But I later saw it in the highlights. You could see Vince Gibson coming back out onto the field, and he looked like a raging bull. It was a cold day. And steam was coming out of his nostrils. I thought, I am glad I didn't see that at the time. He looked so infuriated. But we came out and made a game out of it."

In a game that produced nearly 1,300 yards of total offense, Kansas State also resorted to some trickery on special teams to shock the Tigers, who had a 28–12 lead after a 99-yard kickoff return by Jon Staggers.

Kansas State went on a long drive to narrow the score to 28–18. On the ensuing kickoff, the KSU kicker lined up as if everything were normal and started to approach the teed-up ball. Dickey recalled, "About three yards from the ball, he bent down to tie his shoe. Then another guy came from the side and kicked the ball. Missouri's kick-receiving team had relaxed and Kansas State recovered. Then, on the first play I hit Charlie Collins with a touchdown pass and we had scored two touchdowns in about seven seconds."

Shortly thereafter, Kansas State actually went ahead 31–28, but McMillan and Staggers wouldn't let Mizzou lose. After McMillan connected on a long pass to John Henley, Staggers took the ball to the 1-yard line. Mizzou scored to go ahead to stay, 34–28. Staggers then fielded a punt and dashed 40 yards to the Wildcats' 5-yard line, setting up MU's final touchdown in a 41–38 victory.

"Staggers was running all over the place," Dickey said.

Poppe talked to Dickey about the game years later. "We felt whoever had ball at the end of the game would win," Poppe recalls. "Staggers had a great game. Lynn was a great college quarterback. He was the first real strong passing quarterback we had faced."

Missouri fell behind Oklahoma and Steve Owens, 10–0, the following week. But the Tigers roared back and scored the final 44 points of the game. Heisman Trophy winner Steve Owens kept his 100-yard rushing streak intact, but the Tigers were moving in on their first Big Eight title in nearly a decade.

McMillan's passing took hold in the final three games in a big way. He built up his numbers, as did Missouri's entire offense. He finished with the best single-season passing yards total in school history at that point. The '69 Tigers were then the highest-scoring team in school history after scoring 41, 44, 40 (against

Iowa State), and then 69 against Kansas in the final game, a 69–21 rout of the Jayhawks.

Missouri and Nebraska were co-Big Eight champions with 6–1 records.

"I think in those days it really was a rivalry," Poppe said of the KU game. "That was a game you had to win. And the fact was that they had beaten us the year before. We already knew we were going to the Orange Bowl. We were pretty confident. And they were trying trick plays. One of the things Coach Cooper told me, he used to say, 'Quit thinking and play football.' I was thinking they were using an illegal formation, and I was yelling at officials that it was illegal."

A Chance for the National Title

The situation the Tigers found themselves in 1969 was similar to their situation in 1960. They were a one-loss team, playing in the Orange Bowl against an Eastern power. The major difference in 1960 was that the voting for the national champion was already completed before the Tigers beat Navy, 21–14.

This time Missouri was facing No. 2 Penn State in the Orange Bowl. And if top-ranked Texas lost to ninth-ranked Notre Dame in the Cotton Bowl, it was conceivable a Tigers upset of the unbeaten Nittany Lions, who were also laying claim to the national title, could vault MU to No. 1.

No. 3 Arkansas lost to Mississippi in the Sugar Bowl. No. 5 USC beat Michigan, 10–3, in the Rose Bowl. And remember the Tigers had beaten those same Wolverines by 23 points in Ann Arbor. Ohio State was ranked fourth and had lost to Michigan, costing the Buckeyes their No. 1 ranking and a trip to the Rose Bowl.

The only unbeaten teams left were Texas and Penn State. In a cluster of once-beaten teams and a bowl winner, Missouri could lay claim to No. 1, despite its one-touchdown, mid-season loss at Colorado.

Missouri's Steve Lundholm (left) and Mark Kuhlman tackle Penn State's Charlie Pittman during the fourth quarter of the Orange Bowl on January 1, 1970.

"If Notre Dame had beaten Texas in the Cotton Bowl, then Missouri and Penn State would have been playing for the national championship," Stephenson said. "Ara Parseghian was one of the best recruiters in the history of college football. But he is the worst game-day coach. He shows up with six weeks of practice. What kind of defense did he put out there? A 5–4 defense with four linebackers. The Texas players had played against that since fifth grade. They know how to block it. We are watching the game and they line up in that formation. We said, 'You got to be kidding me.'"

Texas rallied to beat Notre Dame, 21–17. And even if Notre Dame had won, it would have been a moot point because the Tigers suffered a meltdown when they committed nine turnovers in the Orange Bowl. McMillan, from Coral Gables, Florida, threw five interceptions against a star-studded Penn State defense. He also suffered a rib injury early in the game.

There were 19 future NFL players in the game.

"Terry McMillan was trying to throw it deep to Mel Gray," said Mickey Holmes, who worked for the Big Eight Conference. "Mel Gray was a world-class sprinter. But Penn State was playing its defensive backs 25, 35 yards down the field. Don Faurot was still very much involved then. And he came over to where Wayne [Duke, the Big Eight Commissioner] and I were sitting in the press box. He came over and said, 'I can't understand why they aren't trying to throw underneath the coverage.'"

Poppe recounts that bowl game, in which the Tigers out-gained the Nittany Lions, much the same way. "They laid back and played good, hard defense," Poppe said. "It was 10–3 and we were still in it at the end of ball game. It was a long day."

In the late 1990s at a Tigers reunion, Burns remembers that McMillan was finally given a reprieve by Devine for the Orange Bowl loss.

"Devine blamed McMillan for throwing it deep," Burns recalled with a chuckle. "At this reunion, McMillan comes over to us and says, '[Devine] told me after all these years it was not my fault. He told me it was mother's fault for asking for tickets. I am so relieved it was my mom who made him nervous.'"

Burns added, "Devine pushed the panic button early. It was difficult to throw long while it was raining."

Devine's Only Losing Season at MU, Then Exit

The only thing that could exorcise the demons of the loss to Penn State was to start playing games the next season. And the Tigers, despite being unsettled at quarterback, started off 2–0 with an easy 38–0 victory over Baylor in St. Louis and a 34–12 victory over Minnesota in Columbia.

The ninth-ranked Tigers then had their first real test of the season, a matchup against Air Force and splendid receiver Ernie

The team carries Dan Devine off the field after their 35–10 rout of Alabama in the 1968 Gator Bowl. Devine longed for success like this on a higher level, and after the 1970 season departed Columbia to become head coach of the NFL Green Bay Packers.

Jennings back in St. Louis's Busch Memorial Stadium. It was an utter disaster for the Tigers, who fell behind 30–0 at half time. The AstroTurf was wet from a rainstorm and had not been properly drained. Missouri defenders couldn't cut and keep up with Jennings and company on the slick turf.

Air Force, on its way to the Sugar Bowl that season, posted a humiliating 37–14 victory on the Tigers, the most lopsided non-conference loss during the Devine era at Mizzou. As a result, Missouri would never play another football game at Busch Memorial Stadium.

"I remember the wide seams," Burns said. "It was one of first generations of Astroturf. The surface was hard and there was no air in there. It was a terrible place to play football. It was hot."

Burns does remember one light note early that season, showing the curious nature of how Devine's mind worked.

"I was alternating with another tackle," Burns said. "And Coach Devine said, 'Here, give this to [quarterback Mike] Farmer.' He folded a piece of paper. It was a pass play that we had never run. I thought, You would be biggest fool in America if you lose it. I told Farmer, 'Coach Devine said run the play.' He wanted the receivers to run different routes integrated to the play. He just drew it up. Farmer told the receivers where to go."

Missouri rebounded from the Air Force loss to beat Oklahoma State 40–20, but the Tigers' offense would suffer a crippling blow at Nebraska in the next game when Joe Moore went down with shoulder separation and was lost for the season. End of college career.

Moore was well on his way to another 1,000-yard rushing season when he went down with the injury. And Missouri ended up losing to sixth-ranked Nebraska, 21–7—the Tigers' first loss to the Huskers after three straight victories in the series.

"I was scared to death," Burns said. "We had flip-flopped. I was the left tackle and Larron Jackson the right tackle. We were trying to trap the Nebraska tackle. My job was to block down and Larron [would] trap him. But he stunted far to the outside. Joe got a separated shoulder. I was the low man on the totem pole. They didn't chew me out. It was just bad luck. But the next week, we were very competitive."

That was a home game on national television against Notre Dame. Although several Missouri players other than Moore were out with various injuries, the Tigers led 7–3 in the third quarter. Irish quarterback Joe Theismann appeared to be stopped on a third-down play, but he side-armed a completion to end Tom Gatewood past an on-rushing Tiger for a key first down on the way to the go-ahead touchdown in a 24–7 Notre Dame victory.

"Joe Moore [suffered a shoulder injury at Nebraska] and we were unsettled at quarterback," Stephenson said. "Mike Farmer was our best quarterback. But we couldn't play him as much as we could have. There was the Chuck Roper deal. He was from St. Louis. Hank Kuhlmann wanted Roper. Farmer had been at Jefferson City High School when they won 72 straight football games. [Losing Moore] didn't take our heart out. We were 5–6 that year and we played everybody tough."

But for the first time during the Devine era, the Tigers would lose to Kansas State and then to Iowa State—two of those teams you always had to beat, according to Devine. The Tigers led late, 13–10, at Manhattan against Kansas State when Dickey hit a slant pattern for the winning touchdown, 17–13.

"Earlier in the game, I was intercepted right near the goal line," Dickey said. "I threw a bad pass. He was going to return it 100 yards. I knocked him out of bounds and we both rolled up Devine. I remember when he was with the Packers, Devine got hit on the sideline and suffered a broken leg. I remember him saying, 'Man, I haven't been hit that hard since Lynn Dickey.'"

After a 28–13 loss at Oklahoma, the Tigers dropped to 4–5, the first time they had been below .500 after nine games at Missouri under Devine. But Burns remembers the world didn't end.

"A little bit before half time, my wife gave birth to our son," Burns said. "John Kadlec came over and told me she had given birth to an 11–pound, 3–ounce boy. And he was trying to find a faster way for me to get back to Columbia. Afterward, he could have said, 'We have lost this game, forget it.' But he said, 'Your wife is much more important, and delivering a healthy baby.' He is a classy guy."

After the Tigers lost to Iowa State, 31–19, Missouri won what turned out to be Devine's last game as the Tigers coach, 28–17 over Kansas. Excluding the 1960 forfeit by the Jayhawks, Devine had an 8–2–2 record against KU. That's a record his successor Al Onofrio would later envy. Onofrio's failure to emulate that record played a role in him losing his post.

"[Devine] was the type of guy who wanted to move and do better and he moved on to Green Bay," Sam Adams said.

"I think it was kept under wraps, it was a big surprise," Burns added.

On January 14, 1971, the 46-year-old Devine resigned as football coach and athletic director and became general manager/coach of the Green Bay Packers. His statement, as printed in *The Savitar*, the University of Missouri yearbook:

"I would be less than honest if I didn't say that reaching this decision to leave the University of Missouri was the most trying experience of my life. In no way could I have left Missouri for any other college job—and for very few professional opportunities. Speaking for my family, I know we will miss the Columbia community and our friends here very much. Yet ever since I was a youngster I have followed Green Bay football—and for a fellow who grew up in Proctor, Minnesota, this is an opportunity that attracted me greatly."

After 13 years and a lot of great memories and games, it was the dawn of a new era. Former Missouri basketball coach Wilbur Stalcup was named athletic director and Devine's longtime assistant Al Onforio was selected as the head football coach.

chapter 6
Upset Kings

"Al [Onofrio] was probably as good a coach as I ever worked around. He was smart, patient, firm, tough. Players loved him. It was a shame things didn't go better for him."

—Merv Johnson

Offensively Challenged Tigers

The 1971 season at the beginning of the Al Onofrio era was one of the most offensively challenging ones in Missouri history. The Tigers scored just 93 points in 11 games on the way to a dreary 1–10 record—Missouri's first double-digit losing season in history.

In the 1971 Stanford opener, a 19–0 loss, Missouri suffered a shutout in a home opener for only the second time since 1950 as Onofrio went to his third-string quarterback John Venturi in light of the fact both his veterans, Chuck Roper and Mike Farmer, were nursing injuries.

In Onofrio's head-coaching debut, the Tigers' 18 yards rushing were a prelude of things to come for the rest of the season. Kicker Greg Hill was Missouri's leading scorer, but with only 23 points.

In the second game, Missouri lost at Air Force, 7–6, when usually reliable Greg Hill's 37-yard field goal into the wind—with five seconds remaining—was wide. The only victory of the 1971 season came in Game 3, a 24–12 decision over SMU.

In 1971, the Tigers would finish last in the Big Eight in scoring offense, last in total offense, and last in rushing offense. Onofrio's offense was hampered by a quarterback controversy and the lack of a breakaway running threat with the graduation of Joe Moore and James Harrison.

Missouri needed—and would get—some added outside running speed in 1972.

"I said before the season that I didn't know how many games we would win, but that we would have a good football team," Onofrio told *The Savitar*. "But I never dreamed how far we had fallen behind in the recruitment of big-play talent. We have good players at almost every position in our first 22. But what we haven't got are two or three special guys we need."

Overall, Onofrio's first season was an aberration. Things would get better, yet never to the Big Eight championship level. The one thing that was constant: a physical style of football that the MU defense would exhibit even in the first season, when only Nebraska (a 36–0 victory over the Tigers) inflicted a real blowout.

"Al was probably as good a coach as I ever worked around," said Merv Johnson, a Devine assistant coach in 1960–61 and later an Oklahoma assistant. "He was smart, patient, firm, tough. Players loved him. It was a shame things didn't go better for him. The people at Oklahoma remember how badly they would beat them up. [The Tigers] would get in a funny stance. Some of their players were not very big. But you would be black and blue all over after the game. I don't think Onofrio ever did raise his voice. But his players would try to kill you."

While Onofrio's hiring seemed to be popular with assistants and players, it wasn't with everyone.

"When [Devine] left, they went 1–10," said Tom Stephenson, who was a senior in 1971. "That's because the guy was not his hand-chosen. You will never find in *The Kansas City Star* or the *St. Louis Post-Dispatch* where he blessed Onofrio. Sometimes when you hire an assistant coach you get a guy who can't be a head coach."

1972: Not for the Missouri Faint of Heart

The 1972 season would start out with another Pacific Eight team coming to Columbia in the season opener. Oregon quarterback Dan Fouts and the Ducks were in command late and it appeared Missouri might be headed down a path similar to 1971.

Then, after a poor Oregon punt gave Missouri the ball at the Oregon 41 with 29 seconds remaining, first-year quarterback John Cherry completed a 20–yard pass to Jack Bastable. After a seven-yard run centered the ball at the 14, Greg Hill kicked a 31-yard field goal with six seconds remaining. The Tigers had a 24–22 victory at soon-to-be-rechristened Faurot Field.

It was the first of several big field goals Hill, a Columbia, Missouri, native, made during the 1972 season, including the first of three game winners in the closing seconds.

After a loss to Baylor and a victory over California, Missouri's record dropped to 2–2 after a disheartening 17–16 decision to Oklahoma State in Stillwater. The Tigers' normally reliable secondary, on fourth-and-28 and leading 16–10, gave up a 54-yard pass from quarterback Brent Blackman to Steve Pettes. When Oklahoma State kicked the extra point, Missouri was a loser.

The next week, Missouri, hung over from the Oklahoma State loss, was drubbed 62–0 by the Huskers in Lincoln. Missouri gave up 544 yards to Nebraska, had to punt 11 times, fumbled four times (losing three), and had one interception.

A meeting the next week against No. 8 Notre Dame in South Bend appeared ominous for the 2–3 Tigers. The Onofrio regime was definitely on the verge of collapse.

"Bob Devaney could have beaten us 100–0," said Missouri superfan Bill Cocos, who was in attendance in Lincoln. "He took out Johnny Rodgers in the third quarter. Nebraska had one of the best all-around teams those two years [in 1971 and 1972] on offense and defense."

Cocos labels the Notre Dame game the following week as the greatest MU victory of the last half century—and he has seen all of the great ones. Missouri was a 38-point underdog going into the game.

But Missouri looked like a team possessed on the muddy and slippery turf at Notre Dame Stadium. The Tigers scored the first four times they had the ball in the day-long drizzle. Missouri didn't have a turnover or even a penalty until late in the game. Meanwhile, Notre Dame fumbled six times, losing three, and suffered two pass interceptions

"It's a tribute to them," said a stunned Notre Dame coach Ara Parseghian after the game. "It was obvious Missouri was very well prepared. They executed almost perfectly. Except for several delay penalties near the end of the game, they didn't have a single call go against them."

With nothing really to lose after the Nebraska debacle, Missouri was going on fourth down everywhere on the field. Don Johnson, Missouri's 205-pound fullback, rushed for 87 yards and two touchdowns on two short fourth-down plunges. Missouri rushed for 329 yards against a defense that had been yielding only 182 yards a game.

"We thought our backs would have to pick up the load this week," Onofrio told reporters after the game. "We do a good job of going wide and off tackle."

Missouri safety Bob Pankey stole Notre Dame quarterback Tom Clements's first pass. Tiger running back Leroy Moss scored on a 16–yard touchdown. Notre Dame tied the score twice, but the Tigers went ahead 21–14 right before the first half ended.

With Hill connecting on two short third-quarter field goals, the Tigers led, 27–14, going into the fourth and took a 30–14 lead on Hill's final field goal with 10:13 left in the game.

Onofrio said Missouri went to a softer defense when the score got to 30–14 to "to try and prevent the big play."

"When you play Notre Dame, you have to be aggressive and play the percentages," Onofrio said. "This accounted for our attempts to convert fourth-down situations. Our entire line was super, especially the guards, [Scott] Anderson and [Charles] Kirley. I was only convinced we had a victory when we got the ball a final time."

Rev. Edmund P. Joyce, Notre Dame's executive vice president and chairman of the faculty board in control of athletics, visited the Missouri locker room after the game and spoke to the Tigers, as reported in the *Fifth Down*: "What you did today after what happened to you last week is an object lesson to every lad in America. That is what football is all about. You can come back to win. You have every reason to be proud. At Notre Dame today, we know we have been beaten."

Was this a fluke? Obviously not, based on the results of the rest of the season, which would end with a bid to the Fiesta Bowl.

Hill Hits His Stride

Greg Hill was *the* story of the 1972 season. Twice more he would provide game winners for the Tigers in Columbia—a 20–17 victory over seventh-ranked Colorado and an odd 6–5 defeat of No. 12 Iowa State.

Against Colorado, with the score tied 17–17, Hill kicked a 33-yarder with six seconds remaining after John Cherry directed the Tigers on a short drive, with a 17-yard scramble and four-yard sneak of his own, and a 12-yard sweep by halfback Tommy Reamon.

"Missouri had a helluva team out there today," Colorado coach Eddie Crowder said to reporters after the game. "They are certainly not Mickey Mouse. Missouri was better than Oklahoma [a 20–14 loser to Colorado] was last week."

After being mobbed by teammates, Hill remarked: "I never thought I would see light again. We are a lot better football team than a lot of people thought."

"I feel very strongly everything good has to be built on some kind of adversity," Onofrio said. "Our adversity was the Nebraska game. Since that game, we have had two great games. That gives the players confidence.... It is a tribute when you have players who will play as hard as they know how for 60 minutes. You don't win with plays and formations. You win with emotion."

Prior to CU's last possession, Hill had attempted a 22-yard field goal, which was no good. Onofrio said when Hill went out for the first field-goal attempt late in the game, he exclaimed, "Greg, you have to make it!"

After the game, Onofrio added, "I didn't say anything the second time."

Three weeks later, Hill was at it again against Iowa State and big quarterback George Amundson. The Cyclones, under coach Johnny Majors, were having a breakthrough season. And with a 5–2–1 record coming into Columbia, the Cyclones had some momentum, including a 23–23 tie with powerhouse Nebraska.

But Hill washed all that away with his third game-winning field goal when the game was on the line with 1:27 remaining. Hill struck from 22 yards after Cherry directed the Tigers on yet another pressure-packed drive to win a game.

"It seems when pressure is on we play better, make fewer mistakes and start moving the ball," Cherry said.

The game produced no touchdowns, three field goals, and a safety. But Missouri was headed to the Fiesta Bowl after improving to 6–4 with a game with Kansas left. Iowa State was devastated by the loss, stumbled to 5–5–1, but still accepted a bid to the Liberty Bowl.

"I have never been in a stranger game," Iowa State coach Johnny Majors said afterward. "This is a very important loss for me. As a matter of fact, it is the biggest loss I have had as a coach. I told the team earlier in the week that the stakes were getting higher. We had a chance to be third in the conference and go to a bowl game and have the best season we have ever had."

Hill tied the then-Missouri season record of 12 field goals by Henry Brown. Hill was cementing himself as Mizzou's leading scorer for three straight seasons—1971–1973—when he kicked a total of 31 field goals.

"I kick better under pressure," Hill said after the game. "I don't think about it much anymore. We are a completely different team this year. We don't think about the past. They yelled at me, 'This is a bowl bid!' I had a feeling it would come down to me. I told my wife before the game [that] Iowa State would be a tough team. It might come down to a field goal to win."

Missouri finished the regular-season with a 6–5 record and lost to Arizona State, 49–35, in the Fiesta Bowl. The Tigers also defeated Kansas State, 31–14; lost to seventh-ranked Oklahoma, 17–6, in Norman; and were upset in the final game of the 1972 regular season, 28–17, by Kansas.

Over the course of the 1972 season, the Tigers played half of their 12 games against ranked teams and won three of those. Missouri was gearing up for another good season in 1973 as it had developed a solid running game with junior college running backs, including the outspoken and flashy Reamon, who led the Tigers in rushing in both 1972 and 1973.

And Cherry, another junior college transfer, had shored up the uncertainty at quarterback. Onofrio had hired former Oklahoma quarterback Bob Warmack as quarterbacks coach to instill some option plays that would utilize Reamon's speed.

"Missouri has a fleet of backs, as good as you will see," said Colorado's Crowder. "They compare with Oklahoma or anybody. Reamon is good as any back. Their backfield is mostly junior college transfers and they are just now beginning to jell."

Will-o'-the-Wisp: John Moseley

Starting with a 37-yard interception return for a touchdown against Oregon's Dan Fouts in the 1972 season opener, 5'8", 160-pound John Moseley, a walk-on from Columbia's David H. Hickman High School, would demonstrate his ability to make big plays. That was especially true as a punt and kick-off returner.

"As a kid, I looked up to John Moseley," said Dale Smith, a MU defensive end who lettered from 1974 to 1976. "He came from my high school and he had to walk on. He makes All-American between punt returning and defense for a little kid who just wanted to play.

"Kenny Downing [another defensive back from 1973 to 1975] was in the same kind of mold. He was a little guy who was not afraid of anybody. We never had on defense that star kind of quality guy. We had very few defensive stars who went on to the NFL. Our offensive guys did. On defense, mainly it was guys with lesser skill, who had to bring their lunch pail. The high school take on [Moseley]: 'He was a good high school player who was too small to play in college.'"

Nevertheless, in 1973, Moseley, then a senior, was named an All-American for his efforts. He returned 19 punts for 314 yards (an average of 16.5 yards a punt return) and 17 kickoffs for 434 yards (25.5 yards a kick return). And he had a couple of huge punt returns during the regular season.

Missouri started a season 6–0 for the first time since 1960, largely because of Moseley's performance in a 17–7 Missouri victory over 19th-ranked SMU at Texas Stadium in Irving in the

John Moseley was a walk-on who had a knack for making big plays for the Tigers, especially as a kickoff and punt returner. Photo courtesy the University of Missouri

fourth game of the season, and in the game the next week against Nebraska.

An ABC regional television audience watched Missouri and SMU, two 3–0 teams, slug it out with Missouri leading, 10–7, in the third quarter. Missouri stopped the Mustangs' wishbone twice on fourth-and-2 plays in the third quarter.

Then Moseley came up with the deciding play of the game: a 74–yard punt return for a touchdown on the final play of the third quarter. He was actually almost down once, when he put his hand on the turf to regain his balance, but was able to keep going. It was reminiscent of Nebraska's Johnny Rodgers's stunning punt return for a touchdown in the "Game of the Century" against Oklahoma in 1971.

"The punt return by John Moseley took the pressure off us because until then, with our 10–7 lead, we had to play it conservatively," Onofrio said.

The following week, the 4–0 Tigers upset No. 2 Nebraska, 13–12, in Columbia, handing first-year head coach Tom Osborne his first defeat and reversing the 62–0 loss to the Huskers the previous season. Moseley had two long kickoff returns and a late-game interception that ultimately put Nebraska deep in its own territory fielding a punt that was fumbled. Missouri recovered at the Nebraska 4 and scored two plays later.

Osborne gambled on a two-point conversion play after the Huskers scored to make it 13–12. But another one of those lunch-pail MU defenders, back Tony Gillick, came up with an interception after Dave Humm's pass was tipped on the conversion try. That play sealed the victory.

Following a 13–9 victory over Oklahoma State, Missouri entered a game at Colorado with a 6–0 record. It appeared Greg Hill's field goal would be the difference (13–10) before Colorado recovered a Missouri fumble and struck for a touchdown on a quick four-play drive for a 17–13 victory.

Missouri lost four of its last five regular-season games in 1973 and had to settle for a berth in the Sun Bowl, although Moseley was big again in a 14–13 regular-season-ending loss to Kansas when he returned a punt 53 yards to give the Tigers a 13–0 lead going into the fourth quarter. Kansas then struck for 14 fourth-quarter points to beat Missouri for the third straight season under Onofrio.

In the Sun Bowl game, Moseley turned the game in Missouri's favor on the final play of the first half. Auburn had just scored to slice Missouri's lead to 21–10 with eight seconds left. Moseley took the ball at the 16, cut to the left, and then busted up the left sideline untouched for his third touchdown of the season on either a punt or kickoff return.

"It was definitely the key play of the game," Onofrio told the *El Paso Times* about the 34–17 victory over Auburn. "When they scored with eight seconds left, and then we came back to score, it kind of knocked them out of it and really gave us the edge."

Here Comes the Roller-Coaster

From 1974 to 1976, Missouri was college football's biggest enigma.

During that stretch, the Tigers won at Nebraska twice, at Alabama (in Birmingham), at USC, and at Ohio State. And they shut out a powerful Arizona State team in Columbia. But they also lost to inferior Kansas teams twice and were shut out by a mediocre Ole Miss team, hammered by 39 points by Wisconsin, and humiliated by Illinois, 31–6.

"I don't really have an answer," said Jim Leavitt, who was a star defensive back during that era. "We were confident against whomever we played. I vividly remember Alabama, Ohio State, and both times we beat Nebraska up there…. We always played pretty good defense, but offensively we were up and down."

Starting in the 1974 opener with a 10–0 loss at Ole Miss in Jackson, when Missouri remarkably started 22 white players, through a bitter 41–14 loss to Kansas to end the 1976 season, Missouri football was on a roller coaster few will ever forget.

"What happened, Missouri tolerated being 6–5 and beating Nebraska or Notre Dame, and being an upset wonder," Stephenson said. "Dan Devine would not have tolerated that…. You win the games you are supposed to win."

Had Missouri overscheduled with top teams? From 1974 to 1976, the Tigers played 12 nonconference games against Alabama, USC, Ole Miss, Baylor, Arizona State, Ohio State, Wisconsin (twice), Illinois (twice), North Carolina, and Michigan— all teams from major conferences and many of them powers in those leagues.

"We had great ballplayers, but we didn't have enough of them," said Bill Cocos, the MU superfan. "We were playing the Southern Cals, the Michigans, and the Ohio States. We didn't play patsies…. We got different guys hurt."

"We didn't have an enormous strength room," Keith Morrissey said. "Nebraska and Oklahoma were ahead of us. I was only 235 pounds and was on the defensive line…. If we had had a stronger weight regimen…. All their players were stronger and faster. They had a little bit of an edge on us."

But a defensive end on those teams, Dale Smith, believes the tough schedule helped focus Missouri, not hinder the Tigers, who showed inconsistencies inside and outside the conference.

"When you schedule hard early, you practice hard to get ready for them," Smith said. "You do have a game focus. I think it helps with preparation."

What had nothing to do with scheduling was Onofrio's decision that junior college star Tony Galbreath, who later would play in the NFL, shouldn't be his starting tailback in 1974 in that first game against Ole Miss, or that quarterback Steve Pisarkiewicz was not ready to play that early as a sophomore. Those decisions probably contributed to the inconsistent start of the season.

Onofrio awarded his holdover seniors, such as quarterback Ray Smith and running backs Ray Bybee and Bill Ziegler, playing time out of a sense of loyalty. But Galbreath, a star at Coffeyville Community College in Kansas in 1973, had led the junior colleges in rushing with an eye-popping 7.8 yards a carry the previous season. And former MU coach Don Faurot labeled Pisarkiewicz as the "best passing arm to brighten the Missouri scene since the days of Paul Christman (1938–40)," according to the 1975 MU Media Guide.

They were clearly Missouri's stars of the future.

After the 10–0 loss to Ole Miss, Missouri beat Cotton Bowl-bound Baylor 28–21, and shut out No. 7 Arizona State, 9–0, to resurrect the season going into a game against Wisconsin. The 59–20 loss to Wisconsin would serve as the catalyst to get Galbreath and Pisarkiewicz, known as "Zark," more playing time. The headline in the *St. Louis Post-Dispatch* the next morning was "On Wisconsin and on and on and on…."

Given the fickle nature of Missouri football those days, the next week was the Tigers' "up week" when there was absolutely no reason to believe it should be. The Tigers were 21-point underdogs going into the meeting with 12th-ranked Nebraska in Lincoln.

Nevertheless, MU's defense didn't collapse early on the road as it did against Wisconsin. The Tigers did spot Nebraska 10 points, and then waited until 11:26 remaining to make their dramatic turnaround by scoring the final 21 points of the game. Zark got his chance to play late in the third quarter.

Zark threw a nine-yard TD pass to Mark Miller with 4:12 left in the game to push Missouri ahead, 14–10. After an interception by Missouri's Steve Yount took the ball to the Nebraska 5-yard line, Galbreath—who would lead Missouri in rushing in 1974 and 1975—ran it in with 2:29 left for the clinching touchdown in what would be the first of three straight MU victories over Nebraska in Lincoln.

"This was the greatest football game I have ever been associated with," Onofrio said after the game to the *St. Louis Post-Dispatch*. "This one was much better [than Notre Dame]. We snuck up on Notre Dame. You can't sneak up on a traditional rival like Nebraska."

Missouri finished the 1974 season at 7–4 after losing to both Oklahoma and Oklahoma State on the road. A 27–3 season-ending victory over Kansas was the only victory Onofrio would post over the Jayhawks in seven tries. And that fact would be a major factor in his firing three years later.

The Morrissey Factor

ABC Television had concerns about its prime-time season opener between second-ranked Alabama and unranked Missouri to begin the 1975 season. Could Missouri make a game of it? It turned out just the opposite would be true. The Tigers completely dominated the game and posted a shocking 20–7 victory over the No. 2–ranked Crimson Tide at Legion Field in Birmingham.

Alabama would go unbeaten the rest of the season and beat Penn State in the Sugar Bowl.

"You kicked the hell out of us," Alabama Coach Bear Bryant told Onofrio after the game. "It should have been by 40."

Missouri scored all 20 of its points in the first half and was up 20–0 at halftime. Alabama's wishbone, which was run by future New York Jets quarterback Richard Todd, was stopped cold, picking up only 31 yards in the game.

MU defensive end Keith Morrissey, a former high school quarterback from tiny Gallatin, Missouri (graduating class of 36), became a Tigers folk hero with his legendary performance against the Crimson Tide. A sophomore, Morrissey was playing in his first varsity game as well as his first actual game on AstroTurf. He was so unfamiliar with it that he caught his cleats on it as he went on the field the first time.

Morrissey fit right into Onofrio's defensive scheme.

"Al Onofrio in spring practice started to develop a defense that would shut down their offense," Morrissey said. "They executed the wishbone very well and would string out the defense. We played a defense with practically 8–9 guys on the line—the '76 Check'. We played inside the tackle. They were unable to break the initial front or go around the end. They tried the first half.

"Bear Bryant had some problems. He couldn't overcome our defense and he knew Alabama was going to have to throw the ball. The first half I rotated at defensive tackle and shuttled in. I did nothing out of the ordinary."

But Alabama was trailing, 20–0, as Missouri converted on eight of 11 third-down opportunities in the first half. And Tim Gibbons kicked field goals of 44 and 46 yards. Galbreath rushed for 75 yards in the first quarter alone. And he had a three-yard run for a touchdown.

"In the second half they decided to drop back and pass," Morrissey said of an Alabama passing attack that produced 87 yards. "They had built their offense around power. And I was a 235–pound defensive tackle. They had big linemen—280 pounds— who were getting down in the three-point stance [for the running game]. When they stepped back for the drop-back pass, they were not nearly as quick. During a couple of series in the second half, I might have sacked [Todd] three times and stopped a swing pass. The sacks seemed to stop every drive they had."

The small-town Morrissey had made his first plane ride of any kind to the game in Birmingham. But he also made the big-time. He was named *Sports Illustrated* Lineman of the Week for his defensive performance. And he chatted with ABC's sideline reporter Jim Lampley during the late stages of the game.

"He asked me what we were doing to stop them," Morrissey said.

Morrissey added that an ABC Television truck had been positioned in back of the Alabama bench at beginning of the game in anticipation that the Crimson Tide players and coaches would be doing most of the talking after the game. In the second half, it was moved behind the Mizzou bench.

"Al Onforio had the greatest defensive mind," Cocos said. "People didn't know it because he was so quiet.... He whipped Alabama, the wishbone. And he didn't get credit for it."

Galbreath was the offensive star of the Alabama game as he rushed for 120 yards against the Crimson Tide. "Galbreath proved he was one of the best runners in the country," Onofrio said as Missouri jumped from unranked to a No. 5 ranking after the victory over Alabama.

The Tigers played six ranked teams in 1975 and only beat one other, No. 14 Oklahoma State. But they were still in a position to go to a bowl when they entered their last two games with a 6–3 record. A tough 28–27 loss to No. 6 Oklahoma in the 10th game of the season would be a killer blow.

Little Joe's Big Runs

Against Oklahoma, Missouri overcame a 20–0 halftime deficit to take a 27–20 lead with less than five minutes to play in the game in Columbia. The Tigers were probably one defensive stop away from pulling off the upset and one of the great comebacks in Missouri history.

The Sooners' now-slimmer national championship hopes following the previous week's stunning 23–3 loss to Kansas were on the line.

But Joe Washington turned a 4th and 1 into a 71-yard cutback run for a touchdown after taking an option pitch from quarterback Steve Davis. The touchdown sliced Missouri's lead to 27–26.

"Little Joe was fascinating, the way he cut back across the grain because he could run sideways as fast as he could forward," said Dean Blevins, who was an OU quarterback on that team. "He got past one [defender], slipped under another, and the next thing you know he was into secondary and they just didn't catch him."

The huge question is whether or not Missouri's luck was just not with them that day. A key player wasn't on the field for that play in the Tigers' secondary—star Kenny Downing. "He had been knocked silly," Morrissey said of why Downing was on the sidelines.

Oklahoma, needing a win to stay in contention for the Big Eight title and national championship, ran the same play again to Washington on the two-point conversion try. He snuck in right inside the right flag of the south end zone for a 28–27 OU lead and ultimately the victory.

"[Missouri's defenders], they strung it out and strung it out," Blevins said. "He flew into the end zone. It was quite possibly the better run of the two. Missouri fans will tell you that he didn't get in. But if you look at it closely, he did get in."

Missouri, trailing 28–27, wasn't finished. It had one more drive in it to try and win the game. Tim Gibbons, who earlier missed an extra point, then missed a 43-yard field goal that could have won the game.

"Pisarkiewicz had a gun for an arm," Blevins said. "I was standing by Steve Davis on the sideline, and we said, 'This deal is not over.' They were ripping us apart at that time. Missouri fans were into it. They have pretty good fans on the hillside. Missouri was going into that crowd and had a lot of momentum. And I thought they had a good kicker and had a chance."

After that disheartening loss, Missouri's defense didn't show up the next week. The Tigers gave up 626 yards of offense to Kansas, which was a two-touchdown underdog. Jayhawks running back Laverne Smith had 236 yards on 15 carries as KU qualified for the Sun Bowl instead of Missouri with a 42–24 victory in Lawrence.

After the 6–5 1975 season, there was some light speculation Onofrio might be fired, but he was given a one-year contract extension because his original five-year deal had expired. That was hardly much of an endorsement.

1976: The Bigger They Are...

Missouri's 1976 upset victories over No. 8 USC, No. 2 Ohio State, and No. 3 Nebraska—all on the road—might have propelled the team into national title contention. Not this season. Despite compiling a 4–2 record against ranked teams, the Tigers finished 6–5 again and didn't even receive a bowl bid.

Interspersed with the headline upset victories were equally upsetting loses to Illinois, Iowa State, and Kansas—three teams going nowhere. But they all got satisfaction they were spoiling what could otherwise have been a terrific season for Missouri.

USC, Ohio State, and Nebraska all finished in the Associated Top 10 at the end of the season. And the Trojans didn't lose another game that year, winning 11 straight and beating Michigan in the Rose Bowl.

USC's 46–25 loss to Missouri at the Coliseum in Los Angeles was the worst opening-season defeat in school history up to that point. It was the USC coaching debut of John Robinson, the Trojan successor to John McKay, who had become coach of the NFL expansion Tampa Bay Buccaneers.

Tony Galbreath was in the NFL by this point. But Curtis Brown, his replacement and later a Buffalo Bill, scored three touchdowns, one on a 95-yard kickoff return. Brown out-dueled USC's Ricky Bell. And Pisarkiewicz, a senior, completed nine of 16 passes for 171 yards and three touchdowns. The Tigers put away USC with a 17-point second quarter in what was a shockingly easy victory, considering where it was played, who it was played against, and one other problem.

"We had a little plane difficulty and we had to fly down south to get there," Morrissey said of the trip to the West Coast. "Ricky Bell had a good game. But that was a game when our offense broke loose."

Sandwiched in between the USC game and a meeting with Ohio State in Columbus was a game against Illinois in Columbia. The Tigers, who jumped from unranked to No. 6 after the upset of the Trojans, shockingly didn't show up in a 31–6 loss to the Illini. It was just a flat performance.

Missouri's football fortunes were on a yo-yo, even from one half to the next. The next week, the Buckeyes were waiting at the Horseshoe, where Missouri was 0–8–1 in its history. The headline in the *The Columbus Dispatch* that Saturday, September 25: "Buckeyes Face Giant Killer Missouri."

The prospect of an upset appeared slim early in the game. The Tigers trailed No. 2 Ohio State, 21–7, at halftime and appeared to be outmatched against a Big Ten team for a second straight week. Ohio State's massive fullback, Pete Johnson, was on his way to 119 yards rushing before suffering an injury. The joke was he just wore out running against Missouri's porous run defense.

"He was going to get five yards every time he carried the ball," Morrissey said. "We did a lot stunting at the beginning and gave up a lot of yards. It looked like a blowout."

"They had a chance to put it away and didn't get it done," Missouri defensive end Dale Smith said. "You let people hang around and something bad will happen to you."

What made the comeback all the more amazing is that MU's starting quarterback, Steve Pisarkiewicz, had suffered a shoulder injury and the Tigers turned to junior Pete Woods, who was supposed to be redshirted. Woods responded with 106 yards passing and two touchdowns and an additional 86 yards on the ground against the Buckeyes. He looked unfazed.

"Maybe I am just strange, or maybe I will get nervous next week," Woods said after directing Missouri 80 yards with four minutes remaining for the winning points.

With 12 seconds remaining, Missouri's 155-pound junior split end Leo Lewis beat Ohio State cornerback Joe Allegro for a touchdown pass. But it was a close call in the corner. Lewis dropped the ball when he hit the turf, but he held on long enough for the touchdown. "I thought I had blown it," Lewis said afterward.

Trailing 21–20, Missouri went for the victory. Woods called the right play in the wrong formation and then missed connections on a pass play. "I thought it was all over," he said. "Then I saw that flag."

A holding call had been called on Ohio State, giving Missouri a second chance on the two-point conversion. The Tigers made it pay off. From one yard out, Woods snuck over on an option play for the two points and a victory that will forever live in Tigers football lore.

After the game, Ohio State's combustible Woody Hayes chased the officials off the field after the controversial ending and failed to shake Onofrio's hand at midfield.

John Kadlec, Missouri assistant coach for Onofrio in those days, recounted to the Missouri Sports Information Office for an October 2005 special release what had happened off the field.

"That night we're a party at Coach's house and his son answers the phone and it's Woody Hayes," Kadlec recalls. "Of course, Coach didn't believe [him]. But he got on the phone and Woody said 'Al, you beat me fair and square, we did hold that guy and I apologize for not shaking your hand after the game but I want you to know congratulations.' That's pretty good, but Woody had a hot temper."

Missouri's "Boomerooski"

Following wins over North Carolina and Kansas State and a disappointing 21–17 loss to unranked Iowa State in Columbia, the Tigers (4–2 overall) played their third Top 10 opponent of the season on the road, the No. 3 Huskers, as 11-point underdogs. The previous season the Huskers had used the famous

"Bummerooski," a fake punt that turned into a momentum-changing and rambling 40-yard touchdown run by Husker lineman John O'Leary in Nebraska's 30–7 victory in Columbia.

The key play in the 1976 game was named the "Boomerooski" by Missouri players because of its daring nature. Trailing 24–23 and fearful of getting a punt blocked in their own end zone (Nebraska had nearly blocked a previous one), the Tigers coaches elected a long, make-or-break pass from the Missouri 2. It was a stunning call before the national television audience on ABC.

"They faked the dive and threw long to put points on the board," Dale Smith said. "It was one of the better strategy moves I remember."

Quarterback Pete Woods completed a 98-yard pass—still the longest in Missouri history—to Joe Stewart, the Big Eight Conference's leading receiver. The speedy 5'11", 175-pound Stewart was alone at the 35-yard line and took the ball in stride. Nebraska defensive back Larry Valasek came up and tried to keep up with him, but Stewart, with 9.6 speed in the 100-yard dash, separated easily from him. Missouri converted a two-point conversion and Tim Gibbons kicked a 34-yard field goal for the remainder of the scoring.

Nebraska's defensive coordinator, Monte Kiffin, took the blame for the loss after the game: "Twenty-four points is enough to win. We can't give up the long bomb."

In 1976, three of Missouri's last four games were against ranked teams. Missouri lost to No. 16 Oklahoma State, 20–19, and to No. 14 Oklahoma, 27–20, both on the road; and beat No. 14 Colorado, 16–7, in Columbia. For the second straight season, it came down to beating unranked Kansas, this time in Columbia, for a bowl bid. The Tigers were incompetent again, losing 41–14.

"We were very flat against Kansas," Smith said. "We even talked about it being a big game in the papers. They were pretty mediocre.... We played like we were even less."

There was more furor over Onofrio's status after the second straight 6–5 record and disappointing loss to the Jayhawks in the regular-season finale. During the 1976 season, "Fire Onofrio" and

"On with Onofrio" bumper stickers had circulated. The 13-member Intercollegiate Athletics Committee was forced to act after the Kansas game because Onofrio needed a new contract. Onofrio received a three-year deal.

The decision was based on Onofrio's character, the fact Missouri had victories over five bowl teams in 1976, and the team's bright prospects for 1977. MU Chancellor Herbert Schooling commented on the extension at a press conference after the season, as reported in *Missouri Alumnus* magazine: "We wanted to give Al the best possible atmosphere, the best possible conditions in which to work."

Carl Reese had served as an assistant coach at Missouri in 1966 following his playing days. He then left his alma mater, and, after several stops, landed at rival Kansas as linebackers coach in 1975.

"I am at Kansas, and we beat Missouri two years in a row," Reese said. "I am expecting to stay at Kansas and Missouri called and wanted me to come back. I met with Al [Onofrio] in St. Louis. I told him I would love to come back. But I told him, 'There are rumors about you not being on solid ground.' He got mad. He was a great guy, like a father figure. He looked at me and said, 'Get in the car and we are going to Columbia.' We went to see Chancellor Schooling.

"It was a frigid ride. It was right after the season, three or four weeks after we had just beaten them. I wanted to come back. I always want to. I would swim back to him, but they were calling for his job. He walks into the president's office and said, 'I have tried to hire Carl Reese.' The president knew me. We talked about the old days. Al said, '[Reese] is worried about my future.' Schooling looked at me and said, 'As long as I am here, he is my coach.' I went back to St. Louis and I took the job."

Even Schooling didn't foresee what would happen in 1977. Onofrio would last just one more season.

chapter 7
Al's Exit

"Everybody was frustrated, the fans included. We were close, but could never get the edge everybody hoped for."

—Keith Morrissey

Losing Leads to Change

In 1977, Missouri would suffer its first losing season since 1971, which was Al Onofrio's first season as head coach. The 1977 season would cap a 20-year era of the Dan Devine coaching tree and also signal the movement in the athletic director's chair away from Mel Sheehan and toward a more innovative and enterprising personality—Dave Hart.

Change was in the air—but only after a tumultuous 1977 season in which a key injury to star quarterback Pete Woods probably changed the course of Missouri football history. If Woods had been healthy and Missouri posted a winning record, would Missouri's big cigars have been reluctant to dump Onofrio despite frustrations over the roller-coaster nature of his tenure?

Good question.

On a flight from Lincoln, Nebraska, to Kansas City, Missouri, years after he scouted a Nebraska game for a professional team, Onofrio posed that very question to a reporter. It is now up to his players to make that determination—Onofrio passed away in 2004.

"Everybody was frustrated, the fans included," said end Keith Morrissey, the star of MU's 1975 Alabama upset. "We were close, but could never get the edge everybody hoped for. Al Onofrio, in my opinion, had a great mind, and he was a coach who was one of the cornerstones of Dan Devine's success.

"Al was not dynamic personality-wise. He was able to give motivational talks, but he was more comfortable with Xs and Os. And I think people remembered Dan Devine. They unfairly measured Al against him. The Missouri fans would be teased by the great games [of the 1970s]. Expectations rose enormously when we beat those teams."

Unquestionably the defensive mastermind of Missouri's decade of excellence in the 1960s, Onofrio's Missouri tenure would end after 20 seasons, 13 as an assistant and seven as head coach.

Mel Sheehan, a star end for the Tigers from 1946 to 1948 under Coach Don Faurot, was named the MU athletic director in 1972 after a career as a school administrator in St. Louis. He basically was an extension of the Faurot years, which meant few frills and a conservative fiscal policy.

Neither Onofrio nor Sheehan would make the 1978 football season in their positions after Onofrio's messy firing following a disappointing 4–7 record in 1977. Sheehan could not muster enough clout to keep the powerful Kansas City alumni contingent from winning approval for Onofrio's firing following another season-ending debacle, a 24–22 loss to border-rival Kansas.

Onofrio's approval rating—with MU failing to go to a bowl for a fourth straight year—had dropped seriously among fans, even if some of his players were strong supporters.

"Coach Onofrio was a tremendous coach and a tremendous man," said former MU defensive back Jim Leavitt, now the head football coach at South Florida. "He beat a lot of people. I know the last year, it was Pete Woods's senior year, and it was not Al's fault.... I remember we lost to Illinois 11–7 and we fumbled a bunch of times. As a true freshman, Phil Bradley was not ready to play [at quarterback]. Al was a great role model. We were real close."

Woods's Injury Mars Season

Woods, a senior, was expected to be Mizzou's star quarterback in 1977. Before the season could really get started, he suffered a sprained right knee in the opener against USC.

In trotted 18-year-old Phil Bradley from Macomb, Illinois, to face a fourth-ranked Southern California team that had been embarrassed by the Tigers the previous season, 46–25, in Los Angeles.

"I wanted to go back in, but that decision is left to the coaches," Woods said after the game. "I felt I could drop back and throw, but there is no way I could run."

Bradley was having trouble on the exchanges from center, which resulted in fumbles. Still, Missouri made a game of it, slicing USC's lead to 14–10 on a 25-yard field goal by freshman Jeff

Brockhaus in the fourth quarter. USC scored the last 13 points of the game to win going away.

"Going into that kind of situation is something you dream about. I felt we moved the ball pretty well when I was in there, but the turnovers hurt us," Bradley told reporters after the game. "I wasn't totally confident out there because I am new, but that will come with experience. The early fumbles affected my play.... I wasn't worried about interceptions."

The next week, an 11–7 loss at Illinois with Bradley at the controls did nothing to instill confidence in the jittery Missouri offense. Five turnovers killed Missouri against what would be a poor 3–8 Illinois team. It was Gary Moeller's first victory as the Illinois coach. He wouldn't have many of them during a brief three-year tenure in Champaign—six.

It was a ghastly defeat.

"Leo Lewis was back [as a junior] and he had been big, sensational as a freshman," remembers offensive lineman Mark Jones of the humiliating loss. "The offensive line was green and then when we lost Pete; that really hurt us. We had some talented young guys at running back, but we had lost Curtis Brown [after the 1976 season] and Tony Galbreath [after the 1975 season]."

A 28–21 home loss to UC Berkeley the next week was particularly hard to swallow because the Golden Bears beat Missouri with a walk-on quarterback who wasn't even on scholarship. Bradley completed nine of 25 passes for 93 yards and rushed for 92 yards and was showing promise as a leader. But Missouri was 0–3 for the first time since 1956, Don Faurot's last season as the Tigers' head coach.

There was some definite symbolism as it related to Onofrio's job status, although Faurot walked off the sideline on his own. Onofrio wouldn't.

In the fourth game, when Missouri went out to Arizona State and shut out the 20th-ranked Sun Devils, 15–0, in 89-degree heat, there was some temporary relief. But it was an aberration to the season, not the start of the roller-coaster again.

At least Missouri would not start 0–4. And, if the offense was a question mark, at least the Tigers couldn't lose if the other team didn't score. Onofrio's Tigers had actually shut out the normally high-scoring Sun Devils for eight straight quarters over two games, including the 9–0 shutout in Columbia in 1974. Onofrio got the game ball after the Tigers came up with five interceptions, two by Russ Calabrese.

"Arizona State would lose just one other game [during the regular season]," Jones said. "They weren't in the Pac-10 then and didn't have quite the reputation. But Frank Kush was the coach and they did beat Nebraska in the Fiesta Bowl a couple years before."

The next week, there was a dramatic shift in temperatures and game conditions when the Tigers traveled to Ames, Iowa, and Iowa State University. Bradley started the game, but was throwing into a 25-mph wind. Woods came in and ran seven times for minus 38 yards.

"It was my birthday," Jones said. "It was a wretched experience on October 8. Ames can be cold on the Fourth of July. The offensive yards we gained must have been the fewest in the history of the game.

"Iowa State's Mike Stensrud was just massive. I will never forget it," Jones continued. "He was the biggest person I had ever seen in my life. He was 6'5" and the biggest in pro football for a while. We did nothing. He wasn't the only one I couldn't block. Our defense played great. Their running back, Dexter Green, on an isolation lead draw ran into the middle of line, bounced outside, and scored the touchdown."

Final score: Iowa State 7, Missouri 0. It was the first time the Tigers had been shut out in 29 games. Woods also came back the next week and played in a 21–17 loss to No. 7 Oklahoma. He passed for 262 yards and a touchdown. Missouri pulled within the final score, 21–17, and was going in for a winning touchdown when Woods was intercepted by OU's Darrol Ray. The Tigers fell to 1–5 overall and 0–2 in Big Eight and basically were out of the league race before it hardly had begun.

"My knee felt great," Woods said. "I felt like we could score when we needed to, I never really felt like we were stopped offensively. Unfortunately, mistakes stopped us. I really thought we could beat them. I had time to pass and their pass coverage was not as good as some pass coverages that we had faced."

Missouri had 419 yards total offense to Oklahoma's 358. The Sooners manufactured 339 yards on the ground, where quarterback Thomas Lott ran 17 times for 158 yards.

Missouri had won three of its last five games, but it was not enough to save Onofrio's job. Included in that tally was a 24–14 victory at No. 15 Colorado when Woods passed for two touchdowns and ran for another. And again, in a 21–10 loss to No. 11 Nebraska, Woods completed 13 of 26 passes, with two interceptions, in the ninth game of the season.

Woods, whose knee was bruised and battered, wasn't a factor in Missouri's final two games of the 1977 season. Bradley played all the way in a 41–14 victory over Oklahoma State, running 20 times for 108 yards and two touchdowns and passing for 88 yards. The Bradley-led Tigers rallied for three touchdowns in 3:43 in the fourth quarter, wiped out a 14–10 Oklahoma State lead, and registered their biggest point total of the season.

"I like to think of myself as a passer," Bradley said in summing up his freshman season. "But if the situation calls for it, I can put it away and run. My confidence is much better now.... It has been a long season, especially early on. I was coming in with no experience."

In the season-ending 24–22 loss to Kansas, Bradley showed promise again with 93 yards rushing and 91 yards passing. But KU quarterback Brian Bethke had an even bigger day than Bradley did throwing the ball.

Analyzing the Onofrio Years

Bradley would have three more years to cause Big Eight defensive coordinators headaches, but the 56-year-old Onofrio would not be coaching him. The loss to Kansas—Onofrio's sixth in seven years—was too much for the alumni to digest. In most of the cases, the Tigers were favored going into the KU game after a season full of great upsets.

"At that time, in 1977, we were not as competitive as in 1975 and 1976 and we came into the Kansas game 6–4 both those years and they beat us both times," Keith Morrissey said of the Jayhawks denying Missouri two bowl bids. "We [seniors] never competed in a bowl."

Of course, Oklahoma and Nebraska were both national title contenders during the 1970s and went to bowls every year, except when OU was on probation in 1973 and 1974. And the only really weak team in the league was probation-ridden Kansas State. In 1971, Nebraska, Oklahoma , and Colorado finished 1–2–3 in the country, giving way to the slogan "1–2–3…Big Eight."

Between 1970 and 1977, Kansas State was the only league team to fail to go to at least two bowls.

"Remember, the old Big Eight was tough," Missouri superfan Bill Cocos said. "People don't realize how tough it was."

And in retrospect, Missouri played five ranked teams in 1977—USC, Arizona State, Oklahoma, Colorado, and Nebraska—and beat two of those teams (Arizona State and Colorado). The Tigers were really respectable and outright competitive against the rest, despite the unsettledness at quarterback.

The killer losses were the close ones to unheralded teams Illinois, California, and Kansas, when Woods didn't play. If he had played, Missouri could have possibly finished 7–4 and perhaps Onofrio would have retained his job. With an experienced Bradley at quarterback and several outstanding players still there, such as Kellen Winslow, Leo Lewis, Lamont Downer, and a developing defensive backfield that would send several players to the pros, who knows what would have happened in the late 1970s?

But the fact remained that after seven years of Onofrio, Missouri had a 21–28 Big Eight Conference record and his Tigers usually fell into the second tier of league teams when it came to attracting great prospects. And with a Memorial Stadium expansion of more than 10,000 seats set for 1978 and bills to pay for non-revenue sports, any slippage in football attendance would be disastrous.

After a series of meetings between Onofrio and Missouri officials, he was asked to resign by athletic director Mel Sheehan, but wouldn't. So ultimately, Onofrio become the first MU football coach fired since Frank Carideo in 1934.

"I was sitting with Mel Sheehan and he made a statement, a bunch of boosters got together after the Kansas loss in Kansas City," Jones said. "He blamed it on the powerful boosters after another distasteful loss to Kansas and the record with Kansas. Al was about as un-dynamic as could be. He was not a very good speaker. He was not that kind of guy…. It all caught up with him. We had not been to a bowl game for a few years.

"It's funny, you go back to Missouri and it is some big deal we had a Hall of Fame coach. I have never seen a coach held in such high esteem. You would have thought we had brought back a guy who had won a national championship. I think everybody figured it out: he had gotten a raw deal. It was like a president you never liked at time…like Truman. Everybody after the fact wondered, 'Why they'd let him go?' But at the time they weren't that happy."

In November 1977, the day before Thanksgiving, a couriered letter was delivered to Onofrio's home in Columbia. Its message? That he was gone as Missouri's head football coach. After two decades of great service to MU, he was gone.

chapter 8
Phil Bradley Years

"My freshman year, I came here, and I didn't want to play right off. I didn't think I was ready."

—Phil Bradley

Powers Takes the Helm

Warren Powers became Missouri's 27th head football coach in December 1977, after an exhaustive search that included interviews of such coaches as Joe Gibbs, Pat Dye, LaVell Edwards, Larry Lacewell, and Woody Widenhofer—to name a few. But ultimately it came down to Washington State head coach Warren Powers and former Missouri player and assistant coach Merv Johnson as the two finalists.

Johnson, who was assistant coach at Notre Dame under Coach Dan Devine when the Missouri job opened, remembers the MU job search well. The Fighting Irish were coming off a national title season.

"I thought I had the job," Johnson said. "I was surprised and it was really disappointing to me. Warren Powers and I were the final two. I was told there was going to be a press conference on Tuesday and to bring my wife.... I guess it happened for the best."

Powers was the choice. But he would have to pay a $55,000.00 settlement to get out of his Washington State contract after only one year. And he had fashioned just a 6–5 record at Washington State and had lost to Kansas (14–12) in 1977. But Missouri considered all that. Powers had directed Washington State, a college football doormat at that time, to only its second winning season in 12 years.

Plus, Powers had a pro background, having played defensive back for the Oakland Raiders on their 1967 Super Bowl team. He had been associated with a winning Big Eight program as a player under Bob Devaney and as an assistant under Devaney and Tom Osborne at Nebraska. And he had Missouri ties. Powers was a former all-state quarterback at Bishop Lillis High School in Kansas City and his wife, Linda, had attended MU.

Once he got the job, Powers was smart enough to realize he had some talent and the coaches who had recruited it. He retained Carl Reese as defensive coordinator and Clay Cooper as recruiting coordinator off Onofrio's staff.

"I remember Al [Onofrio] calls me in. He was going to get me a job with Steve Sloan, who had just taken the Ole Miss job,"

Reese recalls. "I thought that was going to be my future and what I would be doing. I came back to Springfield [Missouri] and was hanging out. I get a call. And Warren Powers wanted me to be in his office the next afternoon.

"I told his secretary to tell him I didn't need an exit interview," Reese remembers. "She said, 'No, he wants to talk to you about hiring you.' I didn't know him other from him coaching the Nebraska secondary. He hired me on the spot after a 30-minute visit. Warren and [former Reese teammate] Gus Otto had been teammates on the Oakland Raiders. I have always thought Gus Otto helped me get that job."

The Moody Signal-Caller

Phil Bradley was part of that arsenal of talent that Powers inherited. To this day, Bradley remains the most decorated Missouri two-sport star in school history and is the only player to quarterback Missouri to three straight bowls, from 1978 to 1980. The problem for Missouri during the Bradley years was that he preferred baseball over football and had been recruited by the previous staff of Al Onofrio. He was openly hostile to the coaching of Warren Powers.

Bradley's on-the-field and off-the-field questioning of Powers's play-calling and his personal handling was legendary. The Tigers never quite met expectations despite the presence of a galaxy of stars on the team.

The Tigers had some high moments, such as the spectacular 35–31 victory over Nebraska in 1978 that vaulted the Tigers to the Liberty Bowl. But over the three-year period, they squandered great opportunities to win the Big Eight Conference title, particularly during Bradley's junior and senior seasons.

Little did anyone know that the 1978 victory over Nebraska—Missouri's third straight over Nebraska in Lincoln—would be Missouri's last victory over the Huskers for a quarter of a century.

Bradley hailed from from Macomb, Illinois, and was an intriguing figure because he was actually looking for a school that would

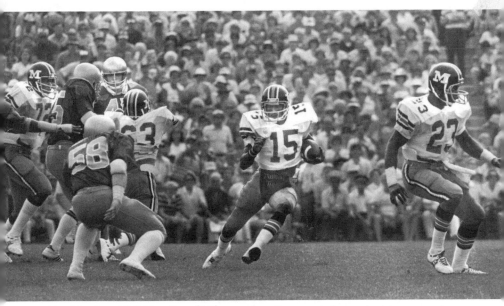

To this day, Phil Bradley (15) remains the most decorated two-sport star in Missouri history and is the only athlete to start at quarterback for the Tigers in three straight bowls (1978–1980). Photo courtesy the University of Missouri

be tailor-made for his baseball skills. He didn't know he could cut it in the Big Eight as a football quarterback, despite the belief to the contrary of MU assistant coach Dick Jamison, who recruited Bradley out of western Illinois.

Ultimately, his future would be as a major-league outfielder with four teams, including the Seattle Mariners, who drafted him. But football was paying most of the scholarship bill at Missouri. Bradley wound up as the Big Eight Football Offensive Player of the Year for three straight seasons (1978–80), despite the fact Missouri failed to win a football title. As a baseball player he was also the 1980 Big Eight Tournament MVP and All-Big Eight and All-American in 1981. Obviously, he was able to pull off the two-sport double with aplomb.

Given the nature of the pecking order sports at major schools, baseball is definitely a second-fiddle sport, especially at a mid-western school such as Missouri.

"With Coach Onofrio in the original recruiting process, Phil had assurances he could play both sports after his freshman year," said Gene McArtor, Missouri's baseball coach in those days. "The typical arrangement was after the first year, he would play spring football. After that, he could play baseball in the spring. Early in his career, he underwent a coaching change. So when Warren Powers came in, Warren was trying to build a football program. And he was interested in seeing him in spring football. Phil had to remind him of his original agreement."

Bradley was just one in a long line of football players who also starred in baseball at MU over the years, including Jack Bastable, Jim Leavitt, Scott Little, Pete Woods, Harold Entsminger, Don Faurot, Bob Haas, Mike Hunter, Charlie James, Hank Kuhlmann, Ed Mehrer, Bob Meyers, Jim Sevcik, John Sevcik, Ray Thorpe, Keith Weber, Paul Christman, Harry Ice, Bob Jeffries, Bob Schoonmaker, Junior Wren, and Butch Houston.

"Football is where the scholarships were," McArtor noted. "Baseball was more limited in scholarship aid than it is today. Baseball was limited in its ability to recruit is own players." McArtor also stressed that spring football was less important early on.

Thrust into a Starting Role

Bradley, as a freshman, was thrust into the fire during the 1977 football season when starting quarterback Pete Woods suffered a sprained right knee in the second quarter of a season-opening home loss to Southern California (27–10). Bradley, 18 years old, replaced him and Missouri had only 234 yards total offense.

"My freshman year, I came here, and I didn't want to play right off," Bradley said in an interview in 1980. "I didn't think I was ready."

After the loss to USC, Bradley was the starter the next week at Illinois. An offensive meltdown occurred in a turnover-marred 11–7 defeat to the rival Illini. It was a particularly stinging defeat for Bradley because it was in front of his home-state fans.

Bradley, along with the rest of the Tigers and their fans, had to struggle through the 4–7 season that cost Onofrio his job..

"Missouri] had difficulty trying to win and there was some social strain off the field," said Mike Price, an assistant coach who came in with Warren Powers. But Price said he had a "great relationship" with Bradley and "he was a very strong kid. He was not a happy-go-lucky camper."

Price remembers one telling moment with Bradley when they discussed his blossoming two-sport career. "He finally looked at me," Price recalled. "He said, 'You love football. I like football. I love baseball.'"

In an interview in the spring of 1980, Bradley left no doubt how he had felt playing for Powers without even mentioning his name: "There have been times the last three years I have thought I should have gone to another school, basically because there have been so many changes in the football program itself...the changes in the coaching staff, that's been the biggest change. Obviously I liked the other coaching staff a lot better because they recruited me. Obviously, it's going to be that way."

One Big Eight Conference office source said that Bradley was miked during one game for a promotional piece and the exchanges between him and Powers were so heated that the production could not be used.

Another Notre Dame Upset

Nevertheless, Bradley's first game under Powers, with Price at his side, was a 3–0 victory at Notre Dame to begin the 1978 season. Powers, a former Nebraska player and assistant coach and a Kansas City, Missouri, native, had been the coach at Washington State for exactly one season in 1977. And Powers led Washington State to a 19–10 stunner against his alma mater, Nebraska, in Lincoln the previous season.

"I remember it was incredibly hot that day at Notre Dame," said Mark Jones, a Missouri offensive lineman. "Most of our coaches smoked and those guys were in there and there was smoke all over the locker room. It was their first game [at Missouri] and they were nervous. The main thing was the goal-line stands. We didn't score a lot of points, but our time of possession was like 10 minutes greater."

The victory over fifth-ranked Notre Dame, Missouri's second straight in South Bend was particularly sweet because it was over former Missouri coach Dan Devine, who was in his fourth season with the Fighting Irish.

It was the first time in 132 games (since a 1965 scoreless tie at Miami, Florida) that Notre Dame had been shut out in any game and the first time the Fighting Irish had failed to score at home since a 21–0 loss to Michigan State in 1960.

For the first time in his career at Missouri, Bradley could just chuckle at the other team having offensive breakdowns against Missouri's fired-up defense.

Three times in the last nine minutes of the game, Missouri's defense stopped Notre Dame on fourth-and-one plays when the Fighting Irish elected not to go for field goals.

"The defense believed in itself and never gave up, certainly putting pressure on [Notre Dame quarterback] Joe Montana," Powers said after the game. "He never had a chance to get on track because our defense kept coming at him. I feel our defense is strong physically. All through the years, Missouri has been a strong-hitting team. I remember [that] when I played against Missouri, they never stopped hitting. When you play Missouri, you better be ready to play."

"I tell you, Coach Devine, bless his heart, he was ash white after the game," said Carl Reese, who had played for Devine at Missouri and was an assistant on Powers's staff. "He had lost all the blood in his body. It was a bitter lick to him."

Missouri defensive back Russ Calabrese said before the game, "I hate all Irish." And the flappy-mouthed Calabrese also came into play during the game, according to Reese.

"Calabrese was a little bit of a hothead," Reese said. "He played the mind. Notre Dame had a great receiver and he was a hothead watching him play. We put Calabrese on his side. And every once in awhile before the play, Calabrese would spit on his shoe. In one of those goal-line situations, Calabrese spits on his shoe. And this guy takes a swing at him [for a personal foul].... That's a true story. If the officials had seen Calabrese spit on his shoe, that's a personal foul. But it's always the second guy they see."

The Notre Dame victory certainly did much to overshadow the off-season talk, which had been devoted to Powers's $55,000 buyout of his Washington State contact. Jokes had been circulating that Missouri would put up collection "garbage cans" around Faurot Field to pay off Powers's contractual debt to his former school by asking fans to donate $1 each.

But what talent Powers had inherited—Onofrio's recruits, basically—was going to be the springboard to four straight bowl trips, three with Bradley at the helm. On the surface, at least, it appeared that Powers had made a good deal.

"We thought we had died and gone to heaven," Price said of the talent at Missouri. "These guys were really good."

"My sophomore year, all I had to do was execute," Bradley said of 1978. "I threw to great receivers and had the [good] offensive line."

Winslow, Other Weapons

Besides Bradley, in 1978 Missouri had such stars as running backs James Wilder and Gerry Ellis, tight end Kellen Winslow, lineman Howard Richards, receivers Leo Lewis and Lamont Downer, and sophomore defensive backs Eric Wright, Johnnie Poe, and Bill Whitaker.

Winslow, from East St. Louis, Illinois, went on to a stellar nine-year NFL career with the San Diego Chargers. He played in five Pro Bowls.

"Winslow hadn't played much in high school, so it was not like he was a veteran player," Price recalled. "But you didn't have to be

Not highly recruited out of East St. Louis, tight end Kellen Winslow would become a star at Missouri on his way to the Pro Football Hall of Fame. Photo courtesy the University of Missouri

a genius to figure out he was a pretty good athlete. We needed to get the ball to him. We weren't a tight end passing team. It would have been a lot different today. Now with the option of routes, Kellen would catch 10 passes a game. He always caught important passes and made big catches. But geez, what would have happened if we had thrown to him 10, 15 times?... We had lots of talent on hand and it was hard to spread the wealth."

Bill Cocos, the Tigers' superfan since 1948, reveals that Winslow, who is one of only two Missouri Tigers in the Pro Football Hall of Fame (along with the St. Louis Cardinals' Roger Wehrli), was not all that high on the Tigers' recruiting list when he brought him to Columbia for a visit in the mid-1970s.

"At that time, alumni could help recruit," Cocos said. "It was not against NCAA rules. We could bring ballplayers to campus.

And we would stay on recruiting weekend. He only played his senior year in high school. I said something to Al about taking a chance. And he had more scholarships available then than they do now…. I would kind of say he was one of the last to go. Kellen probably didn't have that many opportunities to go to Division 1A schools. John Kadlec and I and Vince Tobin were involved."

Winslow became an All-American his senior season.

The Alabama Decision

Missouri had zoomed to No. 11 after the upset to Notre Dame. In the second week of the season, they attempted to make a game of it against the top-ranked Crimson Tide of Alabama. Could Missouri, for the first time in its history, beat top five–ranked teams back to back? Sitting next to Price, who was calling the plays in the Missouri press box, was a high school recruit named John Elway. Jack Elway, John's father, was a personal friend of Price's. The younger Elway was impressed for a half, but, of course, he wound up going to Stanford.

Falling behind 17–0, Missouri rallied for 20 straight points during a scant five-minute period in the second quarter to take a 20–17 halftime lead. However, a bad snap on a punt in the third quarter led to an Alabama touchdown. That play changed the game. Alabama ultimately prevailed, 38–20.

Prior to the punt, the Tigers had a third-and-short call to make a first down.

"We have a third-and-short, and we run just a hard dive with a light back," Jones said. "Gerry Ellis was a much heavier back. [Warren Powers] has always criticized himself…'Why didn't we have a bigger guy carry the ball? Why did we give it to your scat back?'"

In 1978, Missouri also lost to top-ranked Oklahoma (45–23), and was upset by Colorado (28–27) and Oklahoma State (35–20). Following a 48–0 blowout of Kansas, Nebraska in Lincoln was the final game of the season.

"It was a big game, a great atmosphere," Jones said. "It was the kind of game you think of as kid wanting to play in. The coaches did a great job. They had Nebraska ties and believed we could beat them. They thought on the offensive side we could move the ball and we could come up with a good package that would create problems for them. We felt pretty confident.

"It didn't start good for us. We had a lot of opportunities to quit," Jones continued. "I remember counting down the last 50 seconds. And I thought, 'Is it really happening?' [Lineman] Pete Allard was clapping... I thought, 'Didn't we have to run another play?'"

Missouri's 35–31 victory at No. 2 Nebraska was led by Wilder, who scored four touchdowns, including a dramatic goal-line touchdown run when he karate-chopped the hand of a would-be Husker tackler.

"There's a picture of me at end of the play standing up, celebrating over Wilder's touchdown," Jones said. "It was great, without a doubt the greatest athletic moment in my life.

"There was a lot riding on that game," Jones added. "We lose that and we end up 6–5 and there is no bowl game. We win and we are 7–4 and we are infinitely better. We get a Liberty Bowl berth. It is televised by ABC on Saturday afternoon. We are playing LSU from the SEC. We turn around an average season into darned good one."

The Tigers knocked off Louisiana State, 20–15, to finish the season a respectable 8–4. Missouri was in a bowl game for the first time since the 1973 season. Bradley's total offense (with 2,081 yards, including 1,780 passing yards) was key in getting the Tigers to that game.

"He might have been a dentist or sold toothpaste," Reese said of Bradley. "He was low-key. But when it came time to execute and compete, there was nobody better. He was very unassuming and quiet. Before he started, I didn't think he had the spirit or competitive edge. He wouldn't say boo. He was just a great guy. He was one of the reasons Missouri was really good on offense during the early Powers days."

The Wacky 1979 Season

Entering the 1979 season, expectations were high that Missouri would win its first Big Eight title since its 1969 Orange Bowl season. Bradley was back with a year's experience. So was Wilder, who had been a junior college transfer, coming in the season before. The offensive line was experienced. And the defensive backfield was one of the best in the country.

Coach Warren Powers boldly predicted when the Big Eight Skywriters, a group of writers and broadcasters who were previewing league teams, rolled into Columbia, "I think we can win the Big Eight. It's just a matter of going out and doing it. I think our players know they have a great challenge before them. To win the Big Eight you have to play consistent football."

Missouri offensive lineman Mark Jones added, "I really want a minimum of nine wins. I think we can line up with anybody if we play to our potential. Basically, I think we can win 9–10 and maybe 11. This may be my last season of football. It would be a thrill to go undefeated."

Whew! Since Missouri had won nine or more games only twice in modern football history, this was pretty heady stuff coming out of the Tiger camp. Somebody forgot who Bradley might throw to during the 1979 season.

"We didn't have the wide receivers and I had to ad lib a little bit more," Bradley said of missing Lewis, Downer, and Winslow. "I ran 68 yards against Oklahoma for a touchdown. That's not my job. If we had the running backs, I would rather have them do it. I would have been more pleased to have thrown the ball to a receiver and have him run it in for a touchdown."

Bradley's junior season was one of the most perplexing in Missouri history. The Tigers won their first three games—two on the road against Illinois and Ole Miss—and were ranked No. 5 in the country before playing No. 4 Texas. Shut out by the Longhorns 21–0 in Columbia, the Tigers dropped a 14–13 decision to unranked Oklahoma State the following game, in Columbia.

"It doesn't take much to look at our team and say, 'Hey, we haven't jelled the way we had hoped,'" Powers said after the surprising loss to Oklahoma State. "I am as puzzled as the players are as to what is going on."

In the end, Missouri was 5–0 on the road but 1–5 at home, where three of its toughest games—Texas, Oklahoma, and Nebraska—were played. The Tigers lost three league games at home by a total of six points in 1979—by three points to No. 2 Nebraska, two points to No. 7 Oklahoma, and one point to Oklahoma State.

"We never got off the ground offensively," Jones said. "I am being a total armchair quarterback. We were running the same offense as the year before, but we had lost Kellen, Leo, and Downer. We had lost a lot of weapons on offense. Our line was back, and we had James Wilder, Phil, and Gerry Ellis back. So it seemed we should have been better. We were running the split back offense, not the triple option. People stopped the running game and made us throw it. We were decent but couldn't make plays."

There was an even more stunning 19–3 home loss to Kansas State, a team the Tigers had lost to only once in Columbia since 1957.

"Our offense had three points against Kansas State!" Jones said. "At that point, that was a tough loss. That did screw up the whole season. We barely got into a bowl game."

"They were playing like they were looking ahead to Nebraska," said Kansas State free safety Mike Kopsky, referring to Missouri's next opponent.

In his postgame comments, Powers more or less sympathized with the home fans who booed the team during the Kansas State loss.

"I would like to personally apologize to all the Missouri fans for the way the team has been playing lately," Powers said. "Right now we are not a very good football team. That's not to take anything away from Kansas State…they played a very good game. The players are playing as hard as they can, but I must not be coaching very well. The answers are there and we have to find them."

Scoring only three points at home against a team that was a 27-point underdog and was starting a redshirt freshman, Darrell Ray Dickey, the coach's son...well, one can imagine the reaction by Missouri fans. Dickey was terrified when he was warming up before the Columbia crowd.

"I was nervous the previous night," Darrell Dickey said. "L.J. Brown was our running back. He was the coolest guy on the team. Because I was so new, and he was so cool, I sat where he sat during the pregame meal. When I got dressed real fast, I hung around his locker. He said, 'We will be all right.' The whole time I was relaxed. We go into the locker room and come back out. I am not letting him out of my sight. [The Tigers] come out and run toward the center of the field and flip us off. L.J. was looking around and looking into the stands. I thought he would say something that would relax me. He turned to me and said, 'We are getting ready to have the shit beat out of us.'"

But Kansas State used an underneath-passing game against Missouri's tough secondary and came away with the victory when the Tigers' offense stalled.

Missouri (4–3) would have a losing season if it wasn't careful. Bradley figured heavily in keeping Missouri in reach of Big Eight powers Nebraska and Oklahoma. The Tigers lost both games, but led a valiant effort that saw Missouri nearly come back and beat the Huskers in Columbia.

On the final play of the game, trailing 23–20, Missouri was on Nebraska's 11-yard line. Bradley went back to pass, but was flushed out of the pocket by one of Nebraska's ends, who forced an incomplete pass. Jones remembers that he and MU left tackle Dave Guender had some miscommunication regarding the blocking schemes.

"Phil was a good enough athlete to get away [from the end], but if I had blocked it right, he might have had a shot to get in," Jones said. "It was tough anyway. I didn't realize it at the time. But I remember looking at it [on film] and thinking, What the hell!"

Powers said there was no way Missouri would go for a field goal in such a situation. "Our team wasn't ready to play a team like Nebraska for a tie. We needed that win in a bad way to stay in the conference race. I would have never considered going for the field goal unless it was fourth down from around the 25-yard line."

Missouri finished the regular season with a 6–5 record and, despite some criticism of its mediocre performance, accepted a bid to play South Carolina in the Hall of Fame Bowl after the bowl's first choice, Kentucky, lost to Tennessee. Iowa State (5–5–1 in 1972) was the only previous five-loss Big Eight team to go to a bowl.

"I know we may not be the greatest football team," said Bradley, who led the Big Eight in total offense with 160.4 yards a game in 1979. "We had some bad games in the middle of the season. But if the season had started two weeks ago, we would look like a good team. But you can't pick when the season is going to start. You have to be ready on that particular day when the season opens."

In gaining some vindication, Missouri beat South Carolina, 24–14, in the bowl game for Powers's second straight bowl victory.

Coming Close Again in 1980

Bradley's senior football season was solid, but without any spectacular victories. The Tigers weren't tested in their first three games—routine victories over New Mexico, Illinois, and San Diego State. The big-game atmosphere arrived in the fourth game in Columbia when the ninth-ranked Tigers played host to No. 17 Penn State.

Missouri led 21–16 at halftime, then didn't score in the second half. Penn State tacked on two field goals to go ahead 22–21. A 43-yard run by sophomore quarterback Todd Blackledge with 6:17 remaining put the game away, 29–21.

"On the option play, I think our fullback went the wrong way, and their safety keyed off of that," said Blackledge, who was making his first start at quarterback for the Nittany Lions. "And I found myself out in the open. And I ran 43 yards. I had to stiff-arm Eric Wright about the last five yards to get into the end zone. That was by far the longest run I ever had."

Against Penn State, Bradley scored a touchdown on a three-yard run and threw touchdown passes of 31 yards to Ken Blair and 53 yards to Ron Fellows within 1:20 of each other in the second quarter.

"I didn't throw very well in the second half," Bradley said. "I was over-throwing receivers. I was rushing it.... As I look back, the turning point was the drive when we dropped a couple of passes and missed a field goal [late in the second quarter]. We didn't do much after that."

Penn State had suffered a home loss to Nebraska, 21–7, the previous week, leading Penn State safety Pete Harris to observe after the Missouri game, "Missouri compares well with Nebraska. They are a big, physical team with good running backs and a better passing team than Nebraska."

Missouri won eight regular-season games, but was ground up by the Husker rushing machine, 38–16, when I-back Jarvis Redwine punished the Tigers defense for 129 yards and fullback Andra Franklin added 122 in Lincoln. Bradley passed for 229 yards. But the Tigers' ground defense obviously had leaks.

Missouri's other Big Eight loss was to Oklahoma, 17–7, in Norman, when the Sooners rushed for 310 yards. Missouri's offense was stagnant and the Tigers had to punt nine times in Norman.

Thus, Missouri was going to finish out of the throne room again, despite the fact the Tigers would have seven seniors selected in the 1981 NFL Draft: offensive lineman Howard Richards (first round, Dallas), running back James Wilder (second round, Tampa), defensive back Eric Wright (second round, San Francisco), defensive end Wendell Ray (fifth round, Minnesota), defensive back Johnnie Poe (sixth round, New Orleans), defensive back Bill Whitaker (seventh round, Green Bay), and wide receiver Ron Fellows (seventh round, Dallas).

Bradley probably would have gone somewhere in the draft or headed to the Canadian Football League as a quarterback, but he made it known that baseball was his professional future of choice.

While Missouri failed to win even one league football title from 1978 to 1980, Bradley was still named the Big Eight Offensive Player of the Year for the third straight season and finished as the league's career total offense leader with 6,459 yards. After a 28–25 loss to Purdue in the Liberty Bowl, Bradley was freed up to play baseball again, where he hit .457 as a senior.

As a junior, Bradley had been the MVP of the Big Eight Baseball Tournament, which the Tigers won, and in 1981 he was a third-team All-American for the baseball Tigers. He was drafted by the Seattle Mariners, for whom he played through 1987. He also had much shorter stints with the Philadelphia Phillies, Chicago White Sox, and Baltimore Orioles,

Bradley hit 25 home runs in 1985 and was named to the American League All-Star team.

"I don't know that I ever made that projection of anybody," said Gene McArtor, Bradley's Missouri baseball coach. "He certainly had the skill and talent level to take him a long way in baseball. He was an infielder who needed to play outfield to advance his career in baseball. He was special. He had the tools, to be sure. But it depended how hard he would work and improve."

That All-Pro Tiger Backfield

Missouri's 1979 and 1980 defensive backfields were probably the most talented in school history. During those years, the Tigers had four players in the backfield who later would play in the National Football League: Bill Whitaker from Kansas City, Missouri; Eric Wright and Johnnie Poe, both from East St. Louis, Illinois; and, Kevin Potter from St. Louis.

"I knew Wright was a great player," said Carl Reese, who was a Mizzou assistant in those days. "He would break to the ball and knock it dead. He was a safety. He played corner in the NFL.... They were great players. We could play man-to-man or we could play zone. We always played pretty good defense."

The 6'1", 183-pound Wright was the 40th pick overall in the 1981 NFL Draft and played 10 seasons for the San Francisco 49ers. Wright was just one of five players who played on all four of the 49ers' Super Bowl championship teams of the 1980s. As a corner, he had 18 career interceptions in the NFL, including seven in the 1983 season.

The 6'1", 192-pound Poe was selected in the sixth round by the New Orleans Saints, the 144th pick overall in the 1981 NFL Draft. He had 17 career interceptions in seven seasons in New Orleans as a cornerback and safety. His best season was also 1983, when he posted seven interceptions.

The 6', 182-pound Whitaker, who led Missouri with six interceptions in both the 1979 and 1980 seasons, was selected in the seventh round by the Green Bay Packers and played cornerback, linebacker, and safety for four seasons and a total of 39 games. The 5'10", 188-pound Potter played two seasons in Chicago in 1983 and 1984 as a safety.

Dollar Dave: "Show Me" the Money

The most controversial athletic director in Missouri history is Dave Hart, who blew in from the University of Louisville in 1978 like a hurricane swirling dollar signs. His nickname shortly after he arrived: "Dollar Dave."

Because of his controversial donor-ticket policy and his hard-driving sponsorship negotiating, Hart, a fast-talking former University of Pittsburgh football coach, reminded some people of Professor Harold Hill in the hit show *The Music Man*.

The instruments Hart was selling didn't always play in the conservative "Show-Me" State, especially when he came off like a traveling salesman from good ol' Missouri U. Certainly there were those Mizzou alums who wondered if Hart knew his territory.

"I have been a like a new pastor in a church," Hart said in a 1981 interview. "They weren't conditioned. I started passing the basket for donations, and they said, 'Who's this crazy preacher?'"

Hart ruffled feathers from St. Louis to Kansas City and in many small towns in between when he announced in December of 1978 that there would be a $250.00 charge on every seat above two procured in prime football and men's basketball seating areas starting in 1979.

Hart's ticket policy was criticized by Missouri supporters such as Kansas City restaurateur Pete Carter, a longtime buddy of Coach Dan Devine, and Bob Burnes, the influential sports editor of the *St. Louis Globe-Democrat*. But Hart did have one strong supporter at Missouri, former head coach Don Faurot, who understood more than anyone the need to finance the athletic department.

"I am a fan of Dave Hart's," Faurot said in a 1981 interview. "I know there are a lot of old-timers who have a tendency to fight change. And Dave has been rather aggressive in his ticket policies and other things. He has gone after it hard. He has made some enemies from those who have refused to accept change."

"It was explosive," said Jack Lengyel, Hart's associate athletic director at MU from 1981 to 1984 and his successor as MU athletic director in 1986–88. "We did not have the financial support to sustain a major college program. What are your new revenue sources? We were way behind in seat options. Some people had 30 or 40 seats on the 50-yard line."

With rising costs and Title IX requirements for women's sports, many athletic departments were dropping sports or going into the red during the late 1970s. Hart said his ticket policy and increased sponsorship fees were merely instruments to keep MU's athletic department in the black, which he was able to do.

"The premium seat program was exactly the right idea," said Oklahoma athletic director Joe Castiglione, who was a Hart assistant at Missouri. "Dave Hart was well ahead of his time, being innovative and creative and generating new sources of revenue for the program and to help grow the program. They put in a program that has been copied thousands of times. The problem was he was bringing a business approach to a program that really didn't have one. It created a huge, huge problem in implementation. They were essentially forcing people to do something they didn't want to do.

"On top of that, the team wasn't successful and started to decline," Castiglione said of the mid-1980s. "So [the fans] paid more and were getting less, in their minds. It sort of unraveled. It helped the program pay its bills. But as far as public perception, it went off track."

The timing of the first year of the ticket plan couldn't have been worse. The Tigers stumbled to a 1–5 home record in 1979. They won all their games on the road and managed a 7–5 record by beating South Carolina in the Hall of Fame Bowl. But the price to see five home losses had just gone up.

Missouri also went to bowls during the 1980 and 1981 seasons and finished with 8–4 records both years. But the nonconference scheduling began to ease up. In 1981, Missouri's three nonconference home games were against Army, Rice, and Louisville. And in 1982, Army returned for a second game, along with Colorado State and East Carolina. None of those were big names.

"It was a bad combination in hindsight," said Dale Smith, a former Missouri player from 1974 to 1976. "They put the seat licensing in at the same time they were dumbing down the schedule. They built [10,800] additional seats [in the south end zone for the 1978 season]. The supply and demand didn't work. The record didn't support it. And the scheduling didn't support it. If they had played bigger teams, they would have had bigger crowds."

By Powers's final season in 1984 (a 3–7–1 record), during the sixth year of the ticket policy, average home football attendance had dropped to a 13-year low of 47,789. And things didn't get any better under Powers's successor, Woody Widenhofer, who posted four straight losing seasons. Fans had found multiple-choice reasons to stay away.

"The football team started losing and they blamed it on the ticket policy," Hart said of home attendance going down.

"The thing about it, Dave Hart was an innovator, "said MU superfan Bill Cocos. "He kept college sports alive. Non-revenue sports were eating things up when he put that in. Now everybody does it. With our not-so-good record in football, it is unbelievable Missouri football has been in the black."

chapter 9
Powers's Years

"I thought Warren was a good coach. I was always amazed when I would look at his record over time. Why were Missouri fans so impatient?"

—Mark Jones

Starting 5-0 in 1981

For the first time during his Missouri coaching career, Warren Powers entered the 1981 season without Phil Bradley at quarterback. But the Tigers had a nonconference schedule to begin the season that would allow a younger player to feel his way along at the pressurized position.

Missouri opened with three straight home games against Army, Rice, and Louisville. By the end of the 1981 season, those three teams would have a combined record of 12–20–1. It might not have mattered who the MU quarterback was against that trio as the Tigers opened with three home games for the first time since Oregon, Baylor, and Cal in 1972.

The 1981 schedule was a reflection of Powers and MU athletic director Dave Hart, who believed the Tigers' schedules of the 1970s were too tough. In fairness to Hart, Penn State was originally on the Tigers' 1981 schedule, but the Nittany Lions begged off and were eventually replaced by first Temple and then Rice. And Missouri's fourth nonconference game was at Mississippi State, who would be ranked ninth the week the Tigers played the Bulldogs in Jackson.

Compared to the nonconference schedules of the new-millennium teams, Missouri's early 1980s schedule was just pedestrian. Compared to the 1970s Tigers schedules, which included games back-to-back against Notre Dame and Alabama in 1978; USC and Ohio State in the space of three weeks in 1976; and Alabama, Illinois, Wisconsin, and Michigan in 1975, it was much easier.

"I think the schedule has to be balanced," Hart said. "You can't load it up with all with the best in America. You have to have balance and give the coach a chance. When they added a 12th game a few years ago, who did they pick up? Florida State plays Western Michigan in a nonconference [in 2006]. You have got to give the coach a chance."

Parlayed with the football ticket donor policy for prime seating areas that Hart had instituted, the entire scenario left some longtime Missouri fans dissatisfied. Some fans disliked paying extra for the additional prime seats, especially since the opposition was not as attractive.

Nevertheless, the Tigers won their first three games 24–10 over Army, 42–10 over Rice, and 34–3 over Louisville in 1981.

Mike Hyde, who had backed up Bradley and lettered in 1980, was the new quarterback. Faurot Field and more than 60,000 friendly fans provided Hyde an adequate comfort zone. He completed 12 of 20 passes for 189 yards against Army in the opener.

"With the first-game jitters and everything, I am just happy we won," Hyde said after the game. "I can't say what Phil [Bradley] would have or would not have done. I just have to progress with the rest of the team." He completed 17 of 21 passes for 225 yards for four scores against Rice. And he had no problems against Louisville.

In a 14–3 victory over Mississippi State, running back Bobby Meyer had 122 yards on 26 carries, a four-yard touchdown run in the first quarter, and a scoring pass with 1:03 left in the game. Missouri's defense limited ninth-ranked Mississippi State to 237 yards in total offense and a field goal.

"[Mississippi State] took really what we wanted to give them," said Missouri defensive coordinator Carl Reese. "We were taking away the quarterback on the run and making them pass and living with the fullback dive."

MU's defensive linemen Jerome Sally, Randy Jostes, and Jeff Gaylord were swarming Mississippi State quarterback John Bond. And they did the same to Kansas State quarterback Darrell Ray Dickey in a 58–13 victory over Kansas State. In that game, the Missouri offense also produced 393 yards. Gaylord tackled Dickey in the end zone during a 23-point fourth quarter. Gaylord got one of the game balls.

"Maybe this is Missouri's year," Dickey said. "If they give Hyde time to throw the ball, they could beat Nebraska and Oklahoma."

Jeff Gaylord: A Surprise All-American

Jeff Gaylord, a 6'3", 235-pound fifth-year senior, waited until his final season of eligibility in 1981 to really blossom. He had played linebacker, defensive end, and nose guard for the Tigers before landing at defensive tackle the spring before his final season. And he was a hit at the position.

In 1981, Gaylord was named an All-American and led Missouri with eight quarterback sacks for minus 64 yards. His eight sacks in a season was not surpassed at Missouri until the 2000 season when end Justin Smith had 11 quarterback sacks on the way to an All-American season as well. Gaylord was named the MVP of the Tangerine Bowl for his defensive performance when Missouri beat Southern Mississippi, 19–17, after the 1981 season.

Certainly Gaylord was one of the most colorful players in Missouri football history before, during, and after his playing days in Columbia. He was a high school player at Shawnee Mission South High School, in Overland Park, Kansas. Gaylord acknowledged his attitude wasn't always the best in his high-school days.

"I started weight-lifting in the ninth grade," Gaylord said in a 1981 interview. "I was such a brat. Nobody wanted to have anything to do with me." His high-school coach even predicted Gaylord would be limited at Missouri if his attitude didn't change. And his high-school coach looked like he would probably be right through four years.

Before his junior season at Missouri, Gaylord was arrested in a Des Moines, Iowa, bar for indecent exposure. He was performing as a male stripper in a nightclub, stripping down to a G-string.

"All the rest of the guys were professional dancers who did it as a sideline," Gaylord said. "They were all skinny and they wanted a big guy in the show, you know, because people in the audience have different tastes. I was a crummy dancer, but I had the body."

One of the women in the front row pulled down the G-string. Gaylord, who was painted green and dubbed the "Incredible Hulk," pulled them back up. But undercover female cops in the audience arrested him. Gaylord paid a $50.00 fine and continued dancing that summer.

That was just a prelude to a professional wrestling career after his playing days at Missouri, when he bulked up to 280 pounds and used the "Bear Hug" and the "Torture Rack" to win matches during a lengthy career.

Where the 1981 Season Went

Missouri's five-game winning streak ended in Ames, where Iowa State blasted the Tigers, 34–13. The Cyclones were the most balanced team the Tigers had faced. Cyclones running back Dwayne Crutchfield, despite an ankle sprain and leg cramps, gained 98 yards on 32 carries. And Iowa State quarterback John Quinn also passed for 226 yards as the Tigers fell behind, 14–0, and never led.

The following week, in a bitterly cold game in Columbia, archrival Nebraska scored the only points of the game on a three-yard run by fullback Phil Bates with 23 seconds remaining in front of 72,001 fans.

"The kids play their hearts out for 59 minutes," Powers said after the game. "And then to lose it in the last minute, it's really a hard thing to swallow. That's one of the tough lessons of life, I guess. They deserve better than that, but they didn't get it. And Nebraska deserved to win."

Missouri running back Bobby Meyer rushed 15 times for 87 yards and had a long run of 37 yards that he nearly broke for a score. He also had four catches for 38 yards. Meyer's gain of 37 yards took the ball to the Nebraska's 34 early in the fourth quarter, but the drive stalled on fourth down when Hyde's pass fell incomplete.

"We felt we had total control of the line of scrimmage," Nebraska defensive end Jimmy Williams said "We found some weaknesses on the Missouri offensive line [during preparation], which let us know we could put constant pressure on the Missouri quarterback all day."

Missouri lost a third straight game to Oklahoma State, but bounced back with victories at Colorado and against No. 15 Oklahoma, 19–14, in Columbia. MU athletic director Dave Hart then convinced the Tangerine Bowl to invite the Tigers (7–3) before the season finale against Kansas because Missouri had a couple of other bowl options that he might exercise.

The Tangerine Bowl took Missouri without any contingencies of beating the Jayhawks. Then the Orlando-based bowl officials watched in disbelief as KU upset Missouri, 19–11, in Lawrence. KU fans threw tangerines on the field and tore down the goal posts. "Dave buffaloed [the bowl officials]," said Jack Lengyel, a Hart assistant at the time.

Of course, Missouri won the Tangerine Bowl over Southern Mississippi, notching Powers's third bowl victory in four years.

1982: "The Year of the Tie"—And No Bowl

After four straight bowls under Coach Warren Powers, the Tigers would sit home in year five of the Powers regime. The season would be characterized by two ties, questions about Powers's recruiting, and an incident revolving around Missouri defensive tackle Randy Jostes in the Nebraska game.

After routine victories over Colorado State and Army, Missouri was shut out at Texas, 21–0. The Texas loss emphasized the point that great in-state talent was going elsewhere.

In the 1982 Missouri-Texas game, three of UT's prominent linebackers all had Missouri high school ties: June James from Kansas City, Missouri: Jeff Leiding from Hickman Mills, Missouri, by way of Tulsa, Oklahoma; and Tony Edwards from St. Louis. Both Leiding and James would be NFL Draft picks. Edwards was UT's leading tackler as a senior in 1984.

Even so, Missouri still could have gone to a bowl if it hadn't suffered two back-to-back ties in the middle of the season against Kansas State and Iowa State.

The 1982 Tigers were 3-1 going into the Kansas State game. It was a very windy day in Manhattan. This was a much better Kansas State team than previous ones because head coach Jim Dickey had redshirted several seniors-to-be in 1981. Those players were now fifth-year seniors. By the end of the season, Kansas State would go to the first bowl game in school history. Missouri basically allowed Kansas State to get into the game with a botched decision before kickoff. When MU team captains at the middle of the field told officials they wanted to kick off to start the game. Kansas State immediately took the wind.

"I would always talk to our captains," said Jim Dickey. "I would tell them 'You never say "kick." You say, 'We want to defend our end. We want the wind.' Warren came out. The game was delayed five minutes. We had the ball and the wind in the first quarter in a game that ended 7-7. It was vivid in my mind. Warren came out and said, 'We won the flip. There is no way they should get ball and the wind.'"

There were a couple of other bizarre twists in the game. Kansas State's tying touchdown was on a miracle fourth-and-32 pass play from the Missouri 33 early in fourth quarter. Mizzou kicker Brad Burditt tried a 52-yard field goal as time expired to win it for Missouri, but the kick, on-line, was just short. On the previous play, Missouri was penalized five yards for illegal procedure.

The next week against Iowa State, Missouri scored 14 first-quarter points, but only a field goal the rest of the game as the Tigers lost three fumbles and suffered two interceptions in a 17-17 tie with the Cyclones. Over the course of the season, the Tigers were alternating quarterbacks Brad Perry, Mike Hyde, and freshman Marlon Adler trying to find the right offensive spark, but points were hard to come by.

Powers observed after Missouri fell to 3-1-2: "Maybe it's the year of the tie in the Big Eight."

In Lincoln, Missouri came close against fifth-ranked Nebraska, 23–19, before losing. But the focus of the game became a hit by Missouri's Randy Jostes, a Nebraska native, on Husker quarterback Turner Gill. Jostes pushed him away on the play, but Gill's head impacted the turf, causing a concussion that kept him out the rest of the game.

Nebraska coach Tom Osborne told the *Omaha World-Herald*, "It isn't something we should start a civil war over."

While the Jostes story grabbed headlines, the real story at Mizzou was that the Tigers were going nowhere, falling to both Oklahoma and Oklahoma State on the road while beating Colorado and Kansas in the final four games. A 5–4–2 record at Missouri was the fewest number of victories since Al Onofrio's final season of 4–7.

Adler, Hill Come of Age

Missouri's 1983 season got off to a rousing start at Faurot Field, allowing Tigers fans to forget about the offensive problems of 1982. The Tigers smashed Rose Bowl-bound Illinois, 28–18, in a rather stunning opener, considering the hype the Illini had received going into the game.

Sophomore quarterback Marlon Adler looked like an old pro hooking up with former walk-on Andy Hill from Trenton, Missouri. It was a particularly sweet game for Adler, who had won the starting quarterback job from newcomer and much-hyped Warren Seitz and holdover Brad Perry.

Missouri jumped to a 21–0 lead before Illinois could score as Hill caught a 45-yard touchdown pass from Adler that gave MU a three-touchdown lead. The nimble Adler also had a 21-yard run in the fourth quarter for a touchdown.

"Marlon's biggest asset is his versatility," said Hill of the quarterback who would lead MU in total offense each season from 1982 to 1985. "He can run, pass, knows the offense real well. He knows where the guys are, where to look."

Adler also could punt and was the first player in Mizzou history (since punting statistics started being recorded in 1946) to lead the team in punting four straight seasons (1982–85). He had better than a 40-yard average in three of the four years, with a high of 41.9 yards per punt in 1984.

Adler did nearly all he could the next week at Wisconsin as well, scoring three rushing touchdowns. He notched his third touchdown, a one-yard run with 3:41 remaining, to bring MU to 21–20. Missouri elected to go for two points after the touchdown, and Adler's pass intended for Joe Close was incomplete for the win.

Missouri led Wisconsin, 14–7, at halftime. One fumbled Missouri punt set up a second-half Wisconsin touchdown and another led directly to a Wisconsin score that put the Badgers ahead, 21–14, before Adler scored his third touchdown and the Tigers came up just short in Madison.

After a 17–10 victory over Utah State, Missouri was beaten at home by East Carolina, 13–6, a low point of the season. The Tigers were limited to two field goals. Missouri fans wore buttons that read "Where the Hell is East Carolina?"—mocking both the visitors as well as the Tigers for scheduling a game against the team.

Hart said the game had been scheduled before his son, Dave Hart Jr., had become athletic director at East Carolina.

East Carolina running back Earnest Byner, who later would play for the Cleveland Browns, had 16 carries for 95 yards for the Pirates, who scored the game's only touchdown on a 27-yard pass play midway through the final period.

"If someone had told me we wouldn't score a touchdown against a team which has been giving up almost 30 points a game, I wouldn't have believed it," a bewildered Powers said after the game.

Missouri had only 223 yards total offense. Adler was still key in defense, averaging 51 yards on nine punts.

The Tigers salvaged the season with a four-game winning streak (Kansas State, Iowa State, Oklahoma, and Oklahoma

State). The key victory was a 10–0 victory over 11th-ranked Oklahoma in Columbia. Adler and Hill were the combination that basically put the game away with a 20-yard pass for a touchdown in the second quarter

Missouri's defense stifled Oklahoma, forcing the Sooners into two lost fumbles and three interceptions. It took only one big play for Missouri's offense to get the touchdown it needed to win the game.

"Early in the year some of you guys said some nasty things, but maybe that was good for them," Powers said to the media. "They became a little more calloused and believed in themselves. A lesser football team wouldn't be where we are today."

That 20-yard touchdown catch is generally considered the biggest in Hill's career. He also caught 25 passes for 445 yards and three touchdowns in his senior season in 1984, which was also Powers's final season.

"Andy is a player we can depend on in a big game," said Jim Donnan, MU receivers coach at the time. "He will always play as well as he can on every play and that is very reassuring to the coach. Despite his size, he is a big man to his teammates. Everybody knows Andy is going to give 100 percent on every play."

A 37–27 loss to Kansas in Lawrence ended the regular season on a sour note, but the Tigers seemingly were bouncing back in the Holiday Bowl against No. 9 Brigham Young when they held a 17–14 lead in the fourth quarter. They appeared to be going in for the clinching score, but a goal-line stand by BYU stopped the Tigers at the Cougars' 7-yard line with 3:57 left in the game.

Future NFL star quarterback Steve Young then took BYU on the winning 93-yard drive. The capper happened at the MU 14-yard line when Young handed the ball to Eddie Stinnett, who faked running a sweep and threw back across the field to Young for the winning touchdown with 23 seconds remaining for the 21–17 final. MU's Bobby Bell Jr. nearly intercepted Stinnett's pass.

"Young caught one, ran for one, and threw for one," Hart said. "That one kind of got away from [the Tigers]."

Powers's Exit

The 1984 season was one of porous defense and missed opportunities. The Tigers lost three of their first four games by a total of nine points and set the tone for Powers's final season at MU.

The Tigers gave up more points in 1984—301—than any team in previous Missouri history. After a 30–24 opening-season loss at Illinois came a disastrous 35–34 home loss to Wisconsin, where breakdowns in the punting game occurred for a second straight season against the Badgers.

"I was sitting there thinking about last year's game," said MU linebacker Tracey Mack. "I was just hoping the result wouldn't be the same. Unfortunately, it was."

Missouri tailback Vernon Boyd scored from the 6-yard line on a fourth-and-three play with 1:28 remaining in the game. Quarterback Warren Seitz's two-point conversion pass to George Shorthose was dropped by Shorthose. The Tigers' opening-game crowd, 45,033, was the smallest since 1974.

"It was one of those hero to zero plays," Shorthose said after the game.

In 1984, Missouri led 28–7 entering the fourth quarter, but two of Marlon Adler's punts were blocked or altered when Wisconsin used a 10-man line. Missouri couldn't block all the Badgers twice! One of the blocks set up a short Badger drive for a score and the other turned into a score by cornerback Richard Johnson, who also got his hand on the other punt. It was a complete breakdown of Tiger special teams

"We were overloading on one side," Johnson said. "And the up blocker from Missouri didn't pick us up."

In the other close loss, 16–14 to No. 19 Notre Dame, Missouri failed in special teams again before 70,195 fans in Columbia and a national television audience. Brad Burditt missed a 39-yard field goal that would have given the Tigers a much-needed victory over a ranked team.

Missouri's beleaguered defense, which was ranked 91st in the nation going into the game and had given up 95 points in its first three games, actually turned in an inspiring performance. The team donned gold jerseys to honor Coach Don Faurot's final team in 1956. Missouri players were not told about the change prior to receiving the jerseys in the locker room before the game.

The Tigers won only two more games all season, over hapless Colorado and Kansas State. Missouri's home attendance hit a 13-year low. Powers was dismissed with two years left on his three-year contract, which paid him a base of $55,000 a year. Missouri wound up having to pay Powers $110,000 for the additional two years he wouldn't be coaching.

Powers, who had just the one losing season, was a victim of the times. Hart's ticket policy demanded that the Tigers always have winning seasons or the fans would stay away. It was also a time when Oklahoma and Nebraska had powerhouse teams. And in Powers's best years, he could never break their stranglehold on the Big Eight title. After seven seasons, Powers's record was 46-33-3.

"Part of it was Nebraska was really good and Oklahoma was really good," Carl Reese said. "I gave credit to those other teams."

"I thought Warren was a good coach," said offensive lineman Mark Jones. "I was always amazed when I would look at his record over time. Why were Missouri fans so impatient? They treat guys like they do at Ohio State and Texas when they don't win national championships. One season the bottom fell out and they let him go. That doesn't make any sense."

And, as the record would show, Missouri was in for a long drought after Powers left. Including Powers's final 3–7–1 record, the Tigers would go 13 years without a winning record under four different coaches. Missouri went from 1984—Powers's last season—until 1997 without going to a bowl.

"Warren was a good coach," Hart said. "I liked Warren.... We went to five bowls and that's not bad. They were not BCS bowls, but we made money and took people. Missouri traveled well to bowls."

But, as Hart knew, a change was being demanded at the box office.

chapter 10
Woody's Broken Wagon

"When we got Woody, there was a lot of pressure to hire an alumnus. We interviewed every alumnus who ever wore a jock strap.... Well, we got one."

—Dave Hart

Hiring Woody

Missouri went back to its player roots after the final season of the Coach Warren Powers era in 1984. By the start of the 1985 season, the Woody Widenhofer regime was in place in Columbia. Little did Missouri fans know what they were in for in the next four seasons—all losing ones.

The process to determine the successor to Powers was like a Laurel and Hardy movie. There was a lot of slapstick and running around.

How Widenhofer, who was a professional football coach, got the job was purely a reflection of the process. The selection of the new coach was dominated by Missouri chancellor Barbara Uehling, who was going to make sure federal guidelines were followed in opening up the job search to all candidates.

At that time, there was a feeling among the Missouri hierarchy that the Tigers were not going to be a "football factory" in the mold of Oklahoma and Nebraska. This would be reflective in several areas in the coming years, particularly in ever-toughening academic admission requirements for athletes.

So, why not try and waive some of the time period in keeping the job open and hire a coach? Uehling and others at the school would not hear of it. Missouri not only lost several top candidates, it also suffered in recruiting because there was no coach in place for an extended period of time.

What might have happened to Missouri football if any of the coaches interested in the job had actually been awarded it is pure conjecture. Former Missouri assistants and players Carl Reese, Merv Johnson, Vince Tobin, Johnny Roland, and Hank Kuhlmann were among those who had shown interest in the job. They had all distinguished themselves at other schools and/or in the professional assistant-coaching ranks.

"When we got Woody, there was a lot of pressure to hire an alumnus," said Dave Hart, Missouri's athletic director at the time. "We interviewed every alumnus who ever wore a jock strap…. Well, we got one."

Widenhofer was the only one left standing in the prolonged job search because he didn't have a job. He had coached the Oklahoma Outlaws in the United States Football League, but the team had folded and left for Arizona. Widenhofer lettered at linebacker in 1964 for Coach Dan Devine at Missouri and later was an assistant coach for Chuck Noll for the World Champion Pittsburgh Steelers.

He often flashed one his four Super Bowl championship rings—something that obviously impressed the Missouri selection committee. Widenhofer was given credit for coaching the Steelers' famed "Steel Curtain" defense, which included former Missouri player Andy Russell.

"Don Faurot liked Woody very much.... I would have gone to a greater field [other than the alumni coaches]," Hart said. "They wanted to stick to the alumni and Uehling said we have to have an insider.... Andy Russell pushed him a lot.... The board loved him. He was an alumnus and was associated with the 'Steel Curtain.' But it was easy to coach [the Steelers]. I could have come out of retirement."

What Widenhofer had accomplished in the professional ranks didn't translate to the college game, which at the time in the Big Eight was dominated by the option and required intense recruiting, planning, and also some semblance of decorum by the players. Woody would often refer to game day as "Sunday" because of his long standing as a professional assistant. And too often during an inglorious period for Missouri football, his teams appeared to be waiting until the next day to play. Few Missouri players in that era would ever realize professional football dreams.

Ominous Beginning in 1985

Widenhofer's opening game was against Northwestern on September 14, 1985, in Columbia. It proved to be a rather interesting beginning. On the opposite side of the field was Dennis Green, the first African American head football coach in the Big

Ten. He was in his final season at Northwestern, where he would compile a 10–45 record in five seasons before Francis Peay, the former Missouri All-American tackle, would take over the program.

Long before Gary Barnett took the Wildcats to the Rose Bowl, Northwestern was still considered in the dregs of college football. Highly academic, the Wildcats were the Big Ten's version of the Big Eight's Kansas State in that era.

The late Joe McGuff, the highly respected sports editor and columnist for *The Kansas City Star*, just shook his head at this inauspicious beginning of the Woody era. Missouri ended up losing 27–23 to Northwestern. The Wildcats led 17–7 at halftime. MU came back to tie 17–17 after three quarters. Northwestern then got a field goal and touchdown to take a 27–17 lead. Missouri scored with two seconds remaining in the game.

It wasn't the first time Missouri had lost a season opener to Northwestern. It also happened in 1963 (23–12 in Columbia), but those Wildcats went on to post a 5–4 record. The 1985 Northwestern team would finish 3–9.

"We have 10 games ahead of us, it is not going to be easy," Widenhofer said after the 1985 opener. "I really felt bad for our players. I have been through this stuff before. I feel like crying for them. They have made a lot of sacrifices, but in football you need a lot of security. There are a lot of bullet holes in Woody's wagon. In fact, I think it might have fallen apart."

Missouri had 420 yards offense, but gave up 348 yards. Missouri had eight penalties for 59 yards and two passes intercepted. A smallish crowd of 42,221 showed up at Faurot Field—but that would be commonplace for the next decade.

Despite a close brush with victory (21–17) in the second game of the 1985 season against Texas in Austin, the Tigers reverted to an all-too-familiar form in the next game, a 36–17 home loss to Indiana.

The Tigers dropped to 0–6 after losses to Cal, Colorado, and a respectable 28–20 defeat by Nebraska. That set the stage for a loser-lose-all game against another 0–6 team, Kansas State, under interim head coach Lee Moon.

Moon had taken over before the third game of 1985 season after Coach Jim Dickey was fired. Moon would pick up his only victory during a 1–10 campaign against Widenhofer. The Wildcats completed a 49-yard pass on a fourth-and-16 play to set up a touchdown.

"All we had to do was play the ball, don't intercept it, just knock it down," Widenhofer said. "We go for the interception, instead of knocking the ball down. I don't have a lot of answers. It is obvious we are finding ways to lose games, somehow, some way."

That fourth-down conversion seemed to turn the game around and Kansas State rallied from a 17–6 deficit for a 20–17 victory to send Missouri to 0–7 for the first time in school history.

"I thought we had more heart than they did," said Moon, who cried after the game. "Missouri has not been able to hold a lead all year."

The Tigers had a couple of other scoring chances near the goal line and didn't punch the ball in to take control of the game.

"You have to be able to finish them off, if you don't do that you left them off the hook, and they have chance to come back and beat you," Widenhofer said after the game. "The only way that team could beat us is the way they did today—we beat ourselves. If we played them 30 times, we would win 29…. If anybody should take the blame, it should be this coaching staff from me on down."

Widenhofer posted his first win as Missouri coach at Iowa State, 28–27, the following week. Missouri scored with 1:11 remaining to take the lead. Iowa State attempted a 57-yard field goal as time ran out that could have sent the Tigers to 0–8. It was no good.

Woody said to a confidante on the sideline, "If the kicker makes that kick, I will join the priesthood."

He was saved from the clergy, or vice-versa. That would be Widenhofer's only victory during a 1–10 season, which matched Al Onofrio's 1–10 record as his first season as coach in 1971.

Missouri's 1985 team had more penalty yards (639) and penalties (78) than any previous Missouri team. It also gave up more points (342) than any previous team in Missouri history, topping the previous season's opponents' point total.

The OmniTurf Issue

In 1978, Faurot Field was the only field in Big Eight with natural grass. But the addition of the 10,800-seat horseshoe on the south end of the stadium created an airflow problem that contributed to the growth of a fungus that attacked the natural grass and made it a splotchy sight and an uneven surface.

"One thing I have learned is our present turf is not as serviceable as it once was," Widenhofer said at the time. "With inclement weather, our football team needs to be able to practice in the stadium. We want to be able to throw the ball and entertain people. I would have to think artificial turf would be an asset to it."

Widenhofer contended if he was going to recruit the top skilled players, he needed the lure of the speed the artificial turf would allow. Other recruiters used the grass against Missouri.

The sand-based OmniTurf was used at the University of Oregon, without the sand coming up. And according to officials at

After using the controversial—and slippery—OmniTurf at Faurot Field for several years, the Tigers eventually solved their footing problems by bringing back natural grass in 1995.

the Pac-10 school, injuries such as jammed toes, heel bruises, and shin splits decreased.

Jack Lengyel had left Missouri to become athletic director at Fresno State. When he returned to replace Dave Hart in 1986, he inherited the OmniTurf, which was a problem for Missouri.

"It was one of worst turfs ever to come about," said Lengyel, MU athletic director from 1986 to 1988. "Why people were slipping, we were not using the proper cleaning fluid. We finally found what the problem was. But we ultimately went back to grass [in 1995]."

For a decade, Missouri played home games on the slippery surface, including the infamous fifth down game against Colorado in 1990. The Tigers had a 20–39–3 record in home games on OmniTurf.

Getting Help Defensing the Wishbone

The 77–0 loss to Oklahoma in November of 1986 still ranks as the worst loss in Missouri history. The headline in the *St. Louis Post-Dispatch* the next day made reference to the "Norman Conquest." Jokes were made that OU Coach Barry Switzer's staff sent somebody over to the locker room to tell Mizzou defensive coaches how to stop the powerful Oklahoma option.

By halftime, the score was out of control. By the end of the game, Oklahoma had set Missouri opponent single-game records for extra points (11), total offense (750 yards), rushing yards (681), points (77), and tied the record for touchdowns (11).

It was an eye-opening game for Widenhofer during his second season at Missouri. Looking for relief and somebody who could stop the wishbone, Widenhofer called Carl Reese, a former teammate at Missouri and well-respected defensive mind.

Reese had stopped the wishbone before as an assistant at Kansas in 1975 when the Jayhawks had upset powerful Oklahoma, 23–3, during a one-loss season when the Sooners won the national championship.

"That night [after the 77–0 loss] he calls me in Birmingham," said Reese, who was without a job because the Birmingham Stallions of the USFL had folded. "He said, 'Hey, do you know anything about the wishbone?' I told him, 'I promise you I will cut that score in half.' He said, 'You're hired.'"

Because of a lack of speed, Missouri went to a 4–2 defense in 1987 under Reese and played two strong safeties. The Tigers had some tough defenders, but none who could really run. By the next season, Reese had more than fulfilled his promise to Widenhofer when the Tigers again lost to Oklahoma, 17–13, in Norman.

"We should have beaten them," Reese said. "That was a bitter deal. We had several chances to win it."

At the same time he hired Reese, Widenhofer hired a new offensive coordinator, Wright Anderson, to the run the "flexbone," a version of the wishbone. The idea was to control the ball, play good defense, and keep the scores lower. It worked to a degree. Had Missouri beaten Oklahoma, the Tigers would have finished with a 6–5 record in 1987.

Indiana's Hex on Mizzou

Missouri played Indiana eight times from 1985 to 1992 and never beat the Hoosiers, who actually went to five bowls during those seasons under Coach Bill Mallory. Widenhofer and his coaching successor Bob Stull were each 0–3–1 against the Hoosiers, who were improving their middling football reputation at Missouri's expense.

The bad endings against Indiana had an important impact on Widenhofer's four-year tenure. That was particularly the case during his final two seasons (1987 and 1988) when the Tigers appeared incompetent when blowing their chances near the end of each game.

In 1987, the Tigers nearly had the Hoosiers stopped in Bloomington. But on a fourth-and-16 play, Indiana completed a

21-yard pass for a first down that kept the drive alive and took the ball to the MU 27. Three plays later, IU scored on a 25-yard pass play to win, 20–17. Had Missouri won the game, they would have started the season 3–0.

The 1988 Indiana game in Columbia had all the earmarks of a game over which a coach would be fired.

Missouri had tied the score, 28–28, late in the fourth quarter on a 28-yard pass from quarterback John Stollenwerck, a transfer from SMU, to Michael Jones. Indiana had to punt after three plays. The Tigers started a potential game-winning drive at their own 35.

Missouri drove down the field and had a first-and-goal at the 8-yard line, made three yards on a centering running play, and called a time-out to set up a field goal attempt by Jeff Jacke. But he missed a chip-shot, 22-yard field goal attempt when the ball hit the left goal post. The game ended in a 28–28 tie.

"I put my arm around him and said, 'Jeff, sorry it didn't happen,'" Widenhofer said after the game. "I was hoping God would come down and push it over."

Others on the sideline remember that game was the beginning of the end of the Widenhofer regime. Missouri's new chancellor, Haskell Monroe, was a big football fan. And Widenhofer had had some personal problems. So he already was on a short leash.

"The missed field goal, the minute that happened, that was the end of Woody," said Carl Reese, an MU assistant at the time. "We get word after the game. Somebody came and told Woody the new [chancellor] was in the press box throwing stuff and leaving before it was over. [Woody] was a lame duck through the season."

The following week, Missouri was bombed by top-ranked Miami (Florida) on the road, 55–0. The Tigers won only two games the rest of the season, at Kansas State and at Kansas, to finish 3–7–1, the same record Powers had his final season in 1984.

Widenhofer had had four straight losing seasons, however, not just one. In Big Eight play, he had a combined four-year record of

0–16 against Oklahoma, Nebraska, Colorado, and Oklahoma State, the league's first division teams of the era. He had 3–1 records against both Kansas and Kansas State and was 2–2 against Iowa State. Woody's overall record of 12–31–1 was the worst for a Missouri head football coach since the days of Frank Carideo (2–23–2 from 1932 to 1934).

The Tigers football program obviously had slipped. Favorite son or not, Widenhofer was out the door after four unproductive seasons.

chapter 11
Bob Stull Years

"When I took the job, I assumed some things. Really it was my own fault we didn't do better…. There are several things we should have addressed when we got there."

—Bob Stull

Regrouping after Woody

Bob Stull seemed like a natural fit for Missouri's program in the winter of 1988. Few could argue with the success he had had in turning around programs at Massachusetts and the University of Texas at El Paso. The University of Missouri certainly had more going for it than either of those football wastelands. It was only one coach removed from having a winning record in six out of seven seasons under Warren Powers.

Those were the popular theories circulating Columbia as the Tigers tried to claw their way back from the disastrous Woody Widenhofer era from 1985 to 1988.

Haskell Monroe, the University of Missouri chancellor, had been president at UTEP when Stull was head coach in El Paso and took the Miners from the pits of the Western Athletic Conference to the Independence Bowl in 1988. Prior to Stull arriving and posting winning records in 1987 and 1988, UTEP had suffered 16 straight losing seasons, several of the 10- or 11-loss variety.

"Bob Stull was the best hire that year," said Oklahoma athletic director Joe Castiglione, who was an assistant athletic director at MU at the time of Stull's hiring. "He had a great pedigree. It was the third head-coaching job he had taken. And he had taken tough, tough jobs. He turned UTEP and UMass around. That was a really good hire."

Stull also brought a talented staff to Columbia, which included offensive line coach Andy Reid, now the head coach of the Philadelphia Eagles; Dirk Koetter, who was later head coach at Boise State and Arizona State; and Marty Mornhinweg, who was later head coach of the Detroit Lions and now is an assistant coach for Reid in Philadelphia. Stull's background was also linked to the coaching staff of Don James, first at Kent State and then at Washington.

"He was outstanding with people and on his feet as far as addressing people," said Dick Tamburo, the MU athletic director who hired Stull. "He was a people-type person. He was always first class with his recruiting tactics. He was super. I always had faith in him abiding by the rules. He had a fabulous record until he got to Columbia."

What was not factored into the situation was how far Missouri had fallen behind Oklahoma and Nebraska in terms of facilities. Even Kansas State was about to become a power in the league. Academic admission requirements for athletes at Missouri were tougher than other Big Eight schools, lessening the chances of getting even some in-state talent. Even Missouri's nonconference schedule would become a hindrance because of the Tigers' weakened state.

"When I took the job, I assumed some things," said Stull, now the athletic director at UTEP. "Really it was my own fault we didn't do better.... There are several things we should have addressed when we got there.

"Our weight room was 3,000 square feet. We had a real small locker room, offices, and training rooms. We would go out to Texas and recruit and some high schools had weight rooms bigger than ours. Our locker room in the stadium was just concrete and there was no air-conditioning. I never really worried about it. I thought we would win and get people to do what we needed to do. I should have been a guy to say, 'We need this and this to win.'"

Stull said he should have taken the approach Coach Bill Snyder took in building Kansas State into a power. After Snyder dropped a bunch of tough nonconference games, the Wildcats won early in the season and built confidence. By the mid-1990s, Kansas State was a Big Eight title contender.

"And now everybody does it," Stull said. "They won enough games in the conference and won four nonconference games and they would become bowl-eligible.... We would play Texas A&M, West Virginia, Indiana, and then Oklahoma, Nebraska, and Colorado. Really, without a lot of depth it is hard to win that many games."

The other factor that hurt Stull was the tougher academic requirements that Missouri had instituted. The University of

Missouri would not accept non-qualifiers unlike several other Big Eight schools. Missouri's standards required even partial-qualifiers to enroll in English and math courses the summer prior to their initial season of eligibility—at their own expense.

"It was a critical factor," Castiglione said. "A lot of really good players were leaving [Missouri] and going to other universities, most notably KU, Kansas State, Nebraska, and Colorado. They were leaving St. Louis and literally waving at Missouri as they passed by on the way to the other institutions."

Stull also seemed to misjudge what would work in the Big Eight. The league had thrived for years on strong running games and tough run defenses during inclement weather late in the season. Passing was only to keep the defense honest. There had been brief flurries of passing offenses, but Oklahoma and Nebraska, and more recently Colorado and Oklahoma State, had won with strong running games.

Changing MU's Style of Play

Stull came in with a wide-open offense that he had used at UTEP and at the University of Massachusetts. With his Mid-American Conference (Kent State) and Pac-10 (Washington) background, Stull was also used to leagues where passing was more in vogue than in the Big Eight. But he still defends his style.

"It was always funny," Stull said. "They said they were so tired of the running game, 'Let's do something more exciting.' What you like to do is do both. We never really got a great running back. We had decent running backs. We were more pass-oriented. We broke all the [school] records. That was our philosophy. It gave us a chance to compete with people. We did not have the line to pound it down your throat. Eventually, if you are winning, it doesn't make any difference what you do."

The Tigers ran the option offense in Widenhofer's final couple of years, so they needed to find a quarterback to start spraying passes around Faurot Field if Stull's wide-open passing game had any chance of catching hold.

"I think that was such a different style of play for the personnel that weren't on campus," Castiglione said. "It was a tough transition [in 1989]. In 1987 and 1988, we ran the wishbone and an option attack. And here comes a spread-the-field, wide-open passing attack. There was not a quarterback on campus to do it. We went out and got Kent Kiefer."

Dirk Koetter had earlier recruited Kiefer, who had been dissatisfied with his playing time at Arizona State and transferred to a junior college. Kiefer was thrust into the Missouri system in 1989. The transformation was indeed difficult.

In Stull's first season, the Tigers scored more than 21 points just twice, and both of those were losses in Big Eight play, 31–30 to Oklahoma State and 46–44 against Kansas.

In the loss to Kansas, Kiefer passed for 444 yards (at the time the most yards any quarterback had ever passed for against KU). Kiefer's two-point conversion pass failed after Missouri's final touchdown in the closing seconds. Missouri set 11 single-game offensive then-records in that game.

If the Stull era had any kind of trademark, it was the passing and the lack of defense. The latter may have resulted because the Tigers didn't practice as much against a running offense. Over the course of five seasons, the Tigers gave up more than 40 points 17 times in 55 games, or roughly just less than one third of the time.

In 1989, Missouri's defense gave up a record 363 points and scored just 171 points. Missouri's offense would improve under Stull, but the defense really wouldn't until his final season. The 403 points scored against the 1991 Tigers is still a school record for points given up in a season.

"It was always a struggle," Tamburo said. "We were so offensive-minded. I know he changed defensive coordinators one time. We had outstanding kids. But it never kicked in."

The Tony Sands, Iowa State Debacles

In KU's 1989 victory, running back Tony Sands gained 215 yards rushing and scored three touchdowns against Missouri. But that was nothing compared to his 396 yards rushing against Missouri in 1991 in Lawrence. At the time, Sands broke San Diego State running back Marshall Faulk's major-college, single-game rushing total of 386 yards. Sands's mark would stand eight years until TCU's LaDainian Tomlinson gained 406 yards against UTEP in 1999.

"I thought Kansas was trying to run the score up and get him the rushing record," Castiglione said. "Unfortunately, we couldn't stop him."

Sands lugged the ball 58 times, 34 times in the second half when he gained 240 of his yards. In this bitter rivalry, the Kansas coaching staff couldn't help but leave in "Tuxedo Tony" for the record against the Tigers. The 58 carries in a game by one back is still a major-college record.

"When they started flashing those NCAA and Big Eight stats on the scoreboard, you know that even though your team is tired, it gives them something to play for," Kansas coach Glen Mason said after the game. "I hope nobody got mad at me for running Tony that much. The other players were into it on the sidelines. I think that if I had pulled Tony from the game, they would have mobbed me. I wasn't in control, they were."

Stull turned the other cheek, sort of.

"Tony came close enough to the record and they felt they had to give him the opportunity to break it," Stull said. "I think it is all right because 10 years from now no one will ask the question, 'Should the starters be in there at the end?'"

Earlier in the 1991 season, Missouri had lost to Iowa State, 23–22, on a bitterly cold day in Columbia. The windchill factor was 3 degrees below zero, and Iowa State quarterback Kevin Caldwell wore big gloves and completed only one of five passes. He carried the ball 30 times for 154 yards. Yet Missouri never stacked the line or adjusted its defense to stop the run against what had been a passing team coming into the game.

"[Caldwell] won the game for us," Iowa State coach Jim Walden said. "We gave him the chance to run and he it did it very well. He's the only quarterback I have seen wear gloves for all 60 minutes. I don't like running the ball, but if that's what it takes to win, I'd do it."

Stull's End Game

By the 1993 season, the Tigers were looking at a 10th straight losing season. Home football crowds were hovering between 30,000 and 40,000, unless it was for a draw like Nebraska or Oklahoma, which would bring a large number of fans.

"You look at our attendance, even through the bad times, we always had 35,000–38,000," said MU superfan Bill Cocos.

The feel-good vibe of the 1993 season-opening 31–3 home victory over Illinois quickly dissipated with back-to-back road losses to 16th-ranked Texas A&M (73–0) and to West Virginia (35–3). Then came a mistake-filled 10–10 tie against ragamuffin SMU at Faurot Field in the fourth game before the typical crowd of 39,795 fans, who had remained faithful to the Tigers through the tough times.

The tie to SMU was particularly significant because tying or losing to the Mustangs, who had come back from the NCAA's infamous "death penalty" in 1989, was sort of a death knell for coaches. The *Dallas Morning News* pointed out after the 10–10 tie that four of the six previous Division 1A coaches who had failed to beat SMU from 1989 to 1992 didn't return the next season.

Many of the fans at Faurot Field began booing when Stull trotted out kicker Kyle Pooler with 23 seconds remaining to attempt a 47-yard field goal. The Tigers had a fourth and one, with the ability to get closer with 39 seconds remaining, when Stull allowed 16 seconds to run off the clock. Pooler's previous career-long field goal was 38 yards. This one was blocked, the tie was preserved, and the Tigers tumbled to 1–2–1. Missouri never reached .500 again that season, fell to Kansas, 28–0, and finished 3–7–1.

It was Stull's fifth straight losing mark. He never won more than two Big Eight games in a season. With a 15–38–2 overall record, Stull was told in a meeting with MU Athletic Director Dan Devine and Castiglione that he was going to be released.

"Bob Stull took it like a man," Castiglione said. "He was first class in many, many ways. Bob Stull was great and great for Missouri in many ways. He just didn't win enough games. He was very well liked. It disappointed me we had to let him go."

chapter 12
The Fifth Down Game

"When he said 'fifth down,' I just dropped the phone and ran out on the field. At that point Coach Bob Stull is out on the field trying to plead his case with the officials…'You gave them an extra play!' The officials truly did not believe it."

—Joe Castiglione

The Unthinkable Happens

It goes down as one of the most botched sets of officiated plays in college football history and helped determine the 1990 national football championship.

Under circumstances that seem nearly unfathomable today—before thousands of fans and a television audience—a fifth down occurred during a Big Eight Conference game between host Missouri and visiting Colorado on October 6, 1990. It allowed the Buffaloes to score the winning touchdown in the closing seconds of a 33–31 victory at Faurot Field.

With the victory, Colorado eventually claimed the Big Eight Conference title, which automatically put the team in the Orange Bowl, where the Buffaloes beat Notre Dame, 10–9, and claimed the No. 1 ranking in the Associated Press, Football Writers, and National Football Foundation polls. Georgia Tech wound up No. 1 in the Coaches Poll.

The fifth down game has tainted Colorado's national title and created remembrances and memorabilia for those involved. Bob Stull, the Missouri coach at the time and now the University of Texas at El Paso athletic director, for years had a large print of the final sequence, a picture of an official with a fifth-down marker.

Current Oklahoma athletic director Joe Castiglione, who was a senior associate athletic director at Missouri in charge of game management in 1990, has a piece of the turf where Colorado quarterback Charles Johnson landed when he allegedly scored on the fifth down. That's something even Stull and Castiglione dispute—that Johnson actually got over the goal line.

Jack Watkins, the Missouri sports information assistant who was keeping the play-by-play, years later remembers he didn't sleep for two days after the botched officiating sequence, feeling he should have done something from the press box to stop the game from ending that way.

The game is still one of the most talked about in college football history and probably changed the course of Stull's coaching career at Missouri.

"Usually in my career, always by the second year we would get things going," said Stull, whose Tigers finished that 1990 season 4–7 and never did post a winning mark in five years at MU.

"In my second year at Missouri, we had beaten No. 21 Arizona State (30–9) the week before. If we won that game [against Colorado] who knows what would have happened? It gives you momentum. Emotionally, the fifth down game was hard a on a lot of people. More importantly, it changed the focus."

Missouri dropped to 2–3 after the loss. Stull said the following week that all the questions asked of Missouri players were about the infamous ending and news crews were there filming the north end zone where the fifth down occurred. The following Saturday, Nebraska pummeled Missouri, 69–21, in Lincoln.

"That week was something," Stull said. "Sparks were flying there. Those [officials] got suspended. It was not good. It was really embarrassing for everybody in the Big Eight. [J.C.] Louderback will always be known for that. And he was a good official for several years."

Mechanics of the Screw-Up

In the fifth down game, Colorado trailed 31–27 as Johnson, the backup quarterback playing in place of the injured Darian Hagan, directed Colorado deep into Missouri territory. The 12th-ranked Buffaloes, 3–1–1 going into the game, picked up a first down at the MU 3-yard line with 31 seconds remaining. Johnson spiked the ball to stop the clock on first down. On second down, running back Eric Bieniemy carried the ball to the one and Colorado called its final time-out with 18 seconds remaining.

"One of the real interesting things in watching the replay on TV," said Stull, "when they called the time-out and they were on the 1-yard line, [Colorado coach Bill] McCartney got on referee Louderback and told him, 'If we don't get in, make sure they don't lie in the pile. You have to stop the clock if they get up real slow.' When [Bieniemy] goes up on the isolation play and we stuffed him right away, [the officials] stopped the clock…. Conceivably, the clock could have run out."

It is here that communication broke down between the officials on the field and the chain gang.

"Bill McCartney waved Louderback over to his sideline and he talked to him about what would happen if Missouri was slow to get out of he pile," Watkins said. "It was third-and-goal at the 1. But Louderback never told [the chain gang] to flip the marker from second to third down. There was a complete breakdown of communications."

Whether McCartney's waving of Louderback to the side line actually caused the gaffe is debatable, but Watkins said there was no doubt what was being announced in the Missouri press box. Officials failed to flip the down marker to third down when Bieniemy carried the ball for no gain and was thrust backward short of the goal by three Tigers tacklers.

"[Missouri PA announcer] Rod Kelly announced third down from the 1, and Missouri stops them," Watkins said. "It is fourth-and-one and Colorado is out of time-outs. They stop the clock to un-pile. Charles Johnson spikes the ball. We had announced that was fourth-and-goal from the 1. Tom Wheatley from the *St. Louis Post-Dispatch* turns to me and asks, 'Are you sure?' We announce fifth-and-goal from the 1-yard line…Charles Johnson scores."

Adding to the intrigue, the line judge who made the call that Johnson had scored was Terry Turlington, from Kennett, Missouri, a 1967 University of Missouri graduate. Stull says Johnson did not get over, and so does Castiglione.

"Charles Johnson fell on his back," Castiglione said. "Then, after he was down, he took the ball and pushed it over his head. His shoulders were squarely well behind the goal line. He is down. And they called it a touchdown. There were two major issues. It wasn't just the fact they got five downs. They were given a touchdown when they were down, or way before the ball crossed the goal line."

"We have to stop that play and we did," Stull said. "We think we did."

A picture in the *Columbia Daily Tribune* on Sunday appeared to back up those claims. Castiglione was standing on the field as the fiasco developed. After what had been fourth down, when the game should have ended, Castiglione herded security to keep fans off the field and goal posts.

Once Johnson scored on fifth down, Castiglione knew something was wrong. He went over to the sideline phone to call the Big Eight observer in the press box, but Commissioner Carl James had already left the press box to beat the traffic several minutes before and didn't see the last few Colorado plays. Castiglione asked Watkins to read him the play-by-play.

"He said first, second, third, fourth and when he said fifth down," Castiglione said, "I just dropped the phone and ran out on the field. At that point Coach Bob Stull is out on the field trying to plead his case with the officials, 'How could you miss this?' Of course, the Colorado team is celebrating. He is saying, 'You gave them an extra play!' The officials truly did not believe it."

Castiglione said Missouri had no recourse.

"We didn't have instant replay," Castiglione said. "We had television, but it wasn't applicable to the game situation…. [The Missouri coaches] just stood there yelling at the officials…with their hands up…'five downs, five downs'…. The officials truly did not believe they had given Colorado an extra down."

Castiglione said as part of game management, he could go in and visit with the officials after the game. Louderback and the officials conferred for about 20 minutes, but awarded Colorado the touchdown.

"They were stunned," Castiglione said. "It was a great crew. It was a well-respected crew…. They made a mistake. I could tell [Louderback] just looking into his eyes, 'Was there really a fifth down?' he asked. I said, 'Yes, sir, there was.' He was very upset at himself, that they had missed it. He was truly hurt. He was a guy who prided himself on being a tremendous official. Stull handled it with the utmost class and dignity. He also was visibly upset, not so much for himself, but for his team, which had played a terrific game against an excellent opponent and had it taken from them.

"The thing that infuriated Missouri fans more than anything was the way the University of Colorado handled the situation All they could do was complain about the field condition. The OmniTurf was slippery, instead of realizing the turf didn't have any-thing to do with the outcome."

Colorado coach Bill McCartney, who played football for Missouri under Coach Dan Devine from 1959 to 1961, said he considered forfeiting the game. But he didn't do so because he said the field conditions were lousy.

Late into the evening, Stull was doing standup interviews from the stadium with various news outlets about the situation. Watkins said he did not sleep for two days after that game and second-guessed himself for not going down to the nearby coaches' booth where Missouri assistant coaches were to advise them of the situation.

Missouri appealed to the Big Eight Conference to overturn the decision, but the league, citing conference bylaws, declined to do so because it was not a "correctable error."

"That kind of broke our backs that year," said Dick Tamburo. "We lost that thing. And everything went downhill. I was down at the opposite end of the field right toward the end of the game. And they were going north toward the hospital. I didn't realize they had downed the ball once. That is what threw everything off. That hurt the whole program. It was a devastating loss. We played so well. Here we are playing them right out of the stadium and lose."

Anatomy of a Fifth Down

Missouri led Colorado 31–27 before the Buffaloes went on a final drive.

- First-and-goal at MU 3—Quarterback Charles Johnson spikes the ball.
- Second-and-goal at MU 3—Running back Eric Bieniemy runs in the middle for a gain of two. (Colorado takes its final time-out with 18 seconds remaining).

- Third-and-goal at MU 1—Bieniemy runs up the middle for no gain. (Officials stop the clock with eight seconds remaining to clear the pileup.)
- Fourth-and-goal at MU 1—Johnson spikes the ball to stop the clock with two seconds remaining.
- Fifth-and-goal at MU 1—Johnson scores on a run for the Colorado victory. Johnson's run on the PAT attempt failed. Colorado wins 33–31.

chapter 13
The Larry Smith Years

"I really liked Larry. He was organized. He was a fair man. He was energetic. And he was a good person. As an assistant coach, all you want is your head coach to be honest and organized. He would give you a chance to go out there and coach."

—Bill Cubit

Back to the Grind

The hiring of Larry Smith after the 1993 season signaled the return to the running game, eventually a tougher defense, and finally a new grass field at Memorial Stadium.

The architect of the Smith hire was Dan Devine. He had made the Tigers a football power in the 1960s and left to coach the Green Bay Packers and then the Notre Dame Fighting Irish before heading up the substance abuse prevention program at Arizona State University.

In 1992, more than 20 years after he last coached a game at Missouri, Devine had been asked to return to Columbia as athletic director. Devine was to lay a foundation for fundraising and facilities improvements for the now-downtrodden football program at the school.

Part of this process was announcing that Missouri would return to a grass football field by the 1995 season. Another building block for Missouri football was hiring Smith, who was devoted to the running game, option football, and had had successful stints at Tulane (1976–79), Arizona (1980–86), and Southern California (1987–92).

"Larry Smith was out of coaching for a year," said Joe Castiglione, who succeeded Devine as MU's athletic director in 1994. "USC finished 6–4–1 his final season and didn't want to go to a bowl game. So the team voted not to go to a bowl game. But the Pac-10 Conference forced them to go to a bowl and play Fresno State [and they lost, 24–7]. No doubt that is why he got fired."

In some ways, Smith was like Devine. He adored the running game and tough defense, and was more of a CEO type of coach who delegated authority. But recruiting under his predecessor Bob Stull suffered because of lacking facilities and tougher admission requirements. And Smith, trying to rebuild the roster with quality players, suffered three straight losing seasons before he finally turned the corner with Missouri's first bowl season in 14 years in 1997.

Tigers coach Larry Smith shouts instructions to his team during their September 1995 home game against Northeast Louisiana State.

Smith actually suffered more losses in each of his first two seasons (3–8–1 in 1994 and 3–8 in 1995) than Stull did in his last season (3–7–1). The Tigers' defense was a little better through Smith's first three seasons. But the offense was not good enough to push the Tigers' past .500, even in 1996, when Missouri was 5–6.

Nevertheless, Castiglione awarded Smith a two-year coaching contract extension in 1996, valid through the 2001 season, citing that Smith had the program moving in the right direction. With Smith's coaching, coupled with the new facilities' construction under way and more lenient admission standards, Castiglione believed Missouri's program was on the upswing. And it would be in 1997 and 1998.

Missouri's football bowl renaissance coincided with the formation of the Big 12 Conference. Big Eight Conference schools joined Texas, Texas A&M, Texas Tech, and Baylor of the old Southwest Conference to form the two-division behemoth of the midlands, stretching from Ames, Iowa, in the north to College Station, Texas, in the south.

During the Big 12's inaugural 1996 season, Missouri still gave up four touchdowns and 378 yards rushing (third highest total in major-college history at that point) to Iowa State's Troy Davis in a 45–31 loss. But in midseason, the Tigers pulled out a harrowing 27–26 nonconference victory over Southern Methodist University at the Cotton Bowl in Dallas. The turning point came when SMU missed a chip-shot field goal at the end of the game that could have won it.

"This seemed like some of the other games we have played but lost in the last few years," said Missouri wide receiver Rahsetnu Jenkins after the game. "Our luck hasn't been good a couple of times. And it would have been just our luck for the ball to go through the upright instead of bouncing off to the right."

The Corby Jones Ignition

Undoubtedly, junior quarterback Corby Jones was the catalyst for Mizzou, which posted a 7–4 regular-season record in 1997 and accepted a berth in the Holiday Bowl in San Diego, where the Tigers lost to Colorado State, 35–24. Missouri's previous bowl trip, in 1983, had also been to the Holiday Bowl.

"[Smith] turned around 13 straight years of losing," Castiglione said.

And it began with Corby's father, Curtis Jones, who was a former Missouri player in the mid-1960s.

"Curtis Jones was hired by Bob Stull," Castiglione added of the previous MU coaching staff. "Curtis Jones played for Devine and he and Russ Washington were roommates.... Corby transferred in [to David H. Hickman High School in Columbia]. His father came from SMU and went to Missouri. It was between Nebraska and Missouri, the top two choices for Corby."

In 1997, Jones became the first MU quarterback to lead the team in rushing since Gary Lane in 1964.

With the thick grass of Faurot Field and Smith's ground-it-out offense, Jones was a natural. He teamed with methodical senior Brock Olivo, splitting time with talented junior Devin West at tailback, punishing fullbacks Ernest Blackwell and Ron Janes for a fearsome fivesome ground attack. Jones could improvise with his running and was good on play-action passes.

"Corby Jones was kind of an old-school guy," said Duke Revard, a Missouri defensive player during that era. "He was just naturally gifted. He would have been the same player in the '50s as he was in the '90s. He was not a guy who relied on supplements or a real regimented weight program. If you looked at his legs, he was kind of like his dad. They used to say he had old-man

Jay Murchison (81) and Sam Josue (51) are lifted in the air by teammates after they beat Baylor 42–24 in Missouri's final game of the 1997 season. The win propelled the Tigers to a Holiday Bowl berth.

strength. That old, strong, built-up guy, a natural athlete. He didn't need the weight room, all that. He would just kind of show up.

"He was so hard to ever sack. He was kind of slippery. He was so strong. You would grab his jersey and he would pull the other direction. You would kind of fall off. And he would keep going. It wasn't real cat-like quickness. He was just strong. He would have been an athlete in any era. He would have been great in any area as far God-given ability. He worked hard. But he didn't have to work that hard at it, to be as good as he was."

Tragedy hit the Missouri program before Corby Jones's senior season when Curtis Jones suddenly died of a heart attack on July 26, 1998, at the age of 55. But the son persevered and led Missouri to an 8–4 season and a 34–31 victory over West Virginia in the Insight.com Bowl.

In 1998, Missouri led at halftime of every game, including over top-ranked Ohio State in Columbus, before losing 35–14. The Tigers' only losses were to the Buckeyes, No. 7 Nebraska (20–13), No. 6 Texas A&M (17–14), and No. 2 Kansas State (31–25).

Nebraska Game: Flea Kicker

The highlight of the Smith era from 1994 to 2000 may have been one of the most talked-about losses in MU football history. In 1997, the Tigers lost to the top-ranked Nebraska Cornhuskers, 45–38, in overtime at Faurot Field.

"It is probably the most talked-about game around here for the last 13 years," Smith said in 1997. "That last play was a fluke. You just walk away from it. The fact was it was on television and was on nationally in the fourth quarter. We moved light years [ahead] in terms of gaining respect and notoriety for what we have been doing here."

Nebraska, who eventually won the national championship, dropped from the No. 1 ranking after the great escape, and Missouri entered the Top 25 rankings, a rarity after a loss.

"I have heard it called the 'Flea Kicker,' and we have called it the 'Immaculate Deflection,'" Castiglione said. "It was a wonderful game, just a wonderful game. That was a turnaround season. Missouri went on and finished the season and went to the Holiday Bowl. That win would have vaulted them into a major bowl."

Missouri had a 38–31 lead when Nebraska took over the ball at its own 33 with 1:02 remaining. Nebraska quarterback Scott Frost directed the Huskers and had them at the Missouri 10 with seven seconds remaining. Frost threw a hard pass that ricocheted off the chest of NU receiver Shevin Wiggins, whose left leg went up. He kicked the ball to Matt Davison, who caught it before it hit the ground for a touchdown with no time remaining.

"The main thing I remember is that Al Sterling intercepted a pass," Revard said of Nebraska's final drive. "They didn't give it to him. They said he trapped it. It would have ended the drive. That should have ended it. His hands were underneath it. We were in a prevent [defense]. I always hated prevent. That's the only defense people can pass on. If we had just stayed in a blitzing aggressive package...I think we could have shut them down. I remember thinking the game was over [when the final Nebraska pass hit the ground]. The sprinklers went off. And fans started to crowd the field in our end. They thought we had won."

Nebraska scored first in the overtime to win the game.

Smith's Motivational Tricks; Tough Practices

Coach Larry Smith would often reach into his bag of motivational tricks. In 1999, the week before Missouri played Texas Tech, and coming off a 21–0 loss at Kansas, he dropped tennis balls off a tower on the Missouri practice field as part of a "Bounce Back" theme to beat Texas Tech. Missouri won, 34–7.

Smith also had little sayings he would have players tape on their helmets for certain games, such as "You Can Count On

Me"—"YCCOM." And sometimes he had players wearing different colors of jerseys in practice, depending on how they graded out the previous game. Pink jerseys were for poor grades.

On Thursdays of game weeks, after practice, the Missouri starters would take a whack at a boulder near the Tigers practice field with a sledgehammer.

"[Defensive end] Justin Smith would always take off a massive piece of it," MU running back T.J. Leon said. "People were ducking and stuff because the pieces were flying and hitting people."

The Tigers' practices under Smith were Devine-like. No mercy. After a 38–17 loss to Kansas in 2000, the Tigers practiced in pads for four straight days in midseason before going to Austin to play Texas.

"He was mad because we had lost to KU," Revard said. "It was the mentality, 'I don't know what to do, so we are just going to pound each other physically.' It was in the name of going back to the fundamentals. Really, it was just frustration. It just wears you out. I remember Mack Brown's response to what we were doing. In the newspapers he said, 'No pads this week.' And Texas was just as fresh as could be. And Hodges Mitchell breaks out for [151] yards. We didn't have any legs and lost."

The Brock; Tiger Fun and Games

Running back Brock Olivo was Mr. Tiger from 1994 to 1997 and later had his No. 27 retired despite the fact he never rushed for 1,000 yards in a season. He did, however, win the first Mosi Tatupu Award for the best special teams player in the country. And Olivo did have 3,026 rushing yards in his four-year career. Other players considered him a perfectionist in terms of running style, working out, and devoting himself to the Missouri football program under Larry Smith.

"He is a Missouri Tiger," Smith said at the time. "He bleeds black and gold. But he does something about it on and off the field. Here is a guy who has committed himself to Tiger football, not four months of the year, but 12 months of the year. Everything he does, he says, eats, thinks, it's all been Missouri Tiger football."

In a way, Olivo, from St. Francis Borgia Regional High School in Washington, Missouri, embodied the new spirit Smith had brought to Mizzou.

"When I was growing up, Missouri was the doormat of the Big Eight," Olivo told the *Columbia Daily Tribune* in 2003. "That didn't matter to me. The one thing that made me so mad was to see these great players from Missouri commit to Illinois and Kansas and Iowa and Nebraska. There was nothing that got under my skin more. It just hurt me, just got me right in the heart."

Olivo, who started out as a defensive back at Missouri, would take a dare to the extremes as well, like running through four Tigers practice fields nude in the snow.

"I don't know what the weight room looks like now, but they used to have windows lining the whole back," Revard said. "And we had four practice fields in a row, two upper fields and you would drop down, and there were two lower fields. I have seen the video. Some people got some money together [for Olivo] to run all the way down to the fourth practice field naked. It was 300 yards or farther. He's running all the way to the fourth field, butt naked, and I think he is barefoot, too."

One of the common hazing antics of Tigers football in that era was getting "taped up."

"They would take athletic tape and try to hog-tie you with this tape," T.J. Leon said. "I had never seen a guy get taped up until we were coming back from practice. Joe Gianino, a lineman, an Italian, and just a big guy. It was like he was fighting for his life. They had him down on the floor and they were wrestling with him and they were trying to tie his hands and his feet. And he was just going nuts. He had rug burns all over his body when it was said and done. They finally just gave up because he was going so nuts."

Justin Smith: The Slam Tackler

Defensive end Justin Smith, who was a star high school player at Jefferson City High School in Jefferson City, Missouri, became a Tiger All-American his junior season of 2000 and then was a first-round draft choice (fourth overall) by the Cincinnati Bengals in 2001. Over the course of three seasons, Smith sacked opposing quarterbacks 21.5 times for minus-155 yards.

"[Smith] never wrapped-up tackled like you are taught," Revard said. "He would literally do more of the wrestling-style moves. He would body slam people. He would grab them by the neck and bodyslam them. He was known for that."

Revard remembers that Smith could really run.

"We had this return man named Arty Johnson," Revard said. "They called him Arty 'Gym Shoes' Johnson. He was really, really quick. He caught a punt and I was running down with Justin on punt coverage. And Justin got there before everybody else. And Arty put kind of the quickest cat-like move on him and Justin just matched him hip for hip. He just shadowed him. Justin was probably 260 pounds. Arty was probably 150 and one of the quickest guys on the team. When I saw Smitty do that, I thought, 'This guy is an athlete.' He was very, very fluid athletically."

Smith was a man among boys, even as a freshman, when he played for the Tigers. In a 20–6 victory over Oklahoma in Columbia in 1998, Leon remembers Smith manhandling Sooner quarterback Brandon Daniels.

"Oklahoma was running the option play and coming off the edge," Leon said. "The guy was grabbing Justin's jersey. Justin was punching the guy off with one arm. And Brandon Daniels was coming down the line and looked to pitch. He looked back and Justin Smith grabbed him by the neck. I remember him picking him up and just slamming him down.

"Justin was a good ol' country boy coming from Jeff City. He was the kind of guy you could build a defense around. Part of the reason he left was that they didn't have true defensive end in the new system. They were going to be more of a 4–3 defense instead of having a true defensive end. I think that kind of pushed him out the door. Plus, I think he was ready to go."

Smith's Exit

With the graduation of Corby Jones following the 1998 season, Missouri tumbled to 4–7 in 1999 as the Tigers went through several quarterbacks as a result of injuries. And the defense didn't play with the same toughness it had in 1997 and 1998 after Missouri secondary coach Jon Hoke left to become defensive coordinator at Florida under Steve Spurrier. Hoke was generally credited by players as being the brains of the defense.

"Larry was going to change his schemes and go from the option to drop back and throw it a little bit more, " said current Western Michigan head coach Bill Cubit, who was an assistant on Smith's Missouri staff for one season in 2000. "We got hired and went down there. Then the whole thing just blew up in a year and Larry got fired.

"I really liked Larry," Cubit added. "He was organized. He was a fair man. He was energetic. And he was a good person. As an assistant coach, all you want is your head coach to be honest and organized. He would give you a chance to go out there and coach. I have a great deal of respect for him."

Smith's health problems surfaced in 1999, when he was diagnosed with chronic lymphatic leukemia.

"He had some problems with circulation," Leon said. "He actually got to the point he wouldn't stand up during practice in 2000. He would ride that golf cart around. We had really lost a lot of coaches from when I got there in the late 1990s with Coach Hoke leaving and going to Florida. That hurt us and the game changed in the late 1990s. Before it was line-it-up and smash mouth and I think it shifted over to air-it-out."

The pressure had already started to mount on Smith during the 1999 season when, in the last game, Kansas State beat

Missouri, 66–0, in Manhattan. In fact, The Tigers lost their final three games of the 1999 season by a combined score of 154–14. But nobody expected Cheryl Smith, Smith's wife, to come out of the stands in Manhattan.

"I was standing there," Revard said of the blowout loss at Kansas State. "At first [Cheryl] started yelling at the players. Then she started yelling at the refs. She was just angry. I remember Coach Smith trying to hold her back. And he was half embarrassed.... It was understandable she was frustrated. Everybody was frustrated. Everybody felt the same way. Maybe she just lacked some self-control at the moment. She apologized [later to the team]."

And in 2000, the season started going south in the second game during an embarrassing televised 62–9 loss to Clemson.

"The Clemson loss in 2000, they took it off television because it was so lopsided," Revard said. "We started with a bad streak and there was a bad taste in everybody's mouth..... There was a sense of frustration, the coaches blaming the players and the players blaming the coaches."

After a 1–3 start, Missouri won only two more games in 2000 and Larry Smith was gone after seven seasons.

Smith passed away after years of battling leukemia on January 28, 2008. He was 68 years old and living in Tucson, the city in which he had served as the head coach for the University of Arizona from 1980 to 1986. He had other head-coaching stints at Tulane (1976–1979) and the University of Southern California (1987–1992) before ending his career at Missouri.

Smith attended a Missouri football game in Columbia during the 2007 season, celebrating with former players from his 1994–2000 coaching tenure.

"He got Missouri back into bowl games after such a long drought," said Andy Hill, a current Missouri assistant coach who also served under Smith at Mizzou and was a Tiger receiver from 1980 to 1984. "And he will be remembered fondly for that."

chapter 14
The Arrival of Gary Pinkel, Brad Smith

"At the end of the game, I remember [Pinkel] coming in and telling us he is not going to lose and he is not going to allow us to lose. He said we were the worst team he had ever coached…. I could see why he was frustrated."

—T.J. Leon

Jumping from the MAC to the Big 12

Gary Pinkel proved that he could win in the Mid-American Conference at Toledo from 1991 to 2000 when he posted a 73–37–3 record. He was an assistant for Don James during a very successful stint at Washington from 1979 to 1990. Pinkel brought discipline and control to the Missouri program that had run off track in 1999 and 2000.

"When Pinkel came in, he had to change a lot of things," former MU running back T.J. Leon said. "We had a lot of drug-related problems. We lost 15, 16 guys almost immediately when Pinkel came in. We were doing drug tests every week under Pinkel. There had been shadow [weight] lifting under Smith. Guys would come in and do their main power-lift bench and squat and they would mess around and do some curls up front. They had that down to a science."

Pinkel also made players sign contracts about going to class and showing up on time for meetings. If they failed to do so, they would be doing a "lame dog" sort of a bear crawl with one hand. Accountability was at the core of Pinkel's program. Each week, there was a massive board to greet players with their playing grades from the previous game.

"He made it known you were pitted against your peers in every single practice and every single game," former MU linebacker Duke Revard said.

But his former assistant Tom Amstutz, who succeeded Pinkel at Toledo, said this was part of his discipline.

"Gary is a very disciplined coach," Amstutz said. "He really cares about his players. He knows how to run a program, so it is a consistent program. Plus, he gets the most out of his players and he puts them in positions where they can make big plays. So I think he is a tremendous coach."

Bob Stull, Missouri's coach from 1989 to 1993, has a long association with Pinkel that started in the early 1970s. He said Pinkel detests mental mistakes and turnovers.

"Gary Pinkel played for me at Kent State," Stull said. "I was on the coaching staff there. I was the offensive line coach and

New Missouri football coach Gary Pinkel gestures while answering questions on November 30, 2000, during a news conference that announced him as the head coach of the Tigers.

he was a tight end. Nick Saban, Jack Lambert, and Gary Pinkel were tri-captains. When I was at Washington, I was offensive coordinator and he was the receivers coach. When I left he became coordinator. Gary was with Don James when they went to three or four Rose Bowls…. They act like he has never been around."

Revard said Smith's practices, however, were more grueling than Pinkel's.

"Larry Smith was big on full contact, really physical practices," Revard said. "We would just beat the tar out of each other for two hours. Pinkel was much more finesse. Pinkel thought his practices were harder. He used to come in and say, 'I am going to practice you guys like you have never been practiced before.' His thought was we were slacking off and in the Smith era we were lazy and laying around…. Pinkel would say how much harder it was going to be, but we thought it was a lot easier. Ricky Hunley, under Smith he was the linebackers coach. He was the most ruthless conditioner. He would put us through the ringer. People would be throwing up."

Brad Smith Makes Believers of Big 12 Opponents

Without big-time playmakers in his first season in 2001, Pinkel's system provided only one more victory (4–7) than the previous season under Larry Smith. But that was all about to change with quarterback Brad Smith from Youngstown, Ohio. In four years, he would set 69 different Missouri, Big 12, and NCAA game, season, and career records. Smith sat out Pinkel's first season at MU as a redshirt freshman in 2001.

By the 2002 season opener against Illinois in St. Louis, Smith had won the starting job from often-injured senior Kirk Farmer. For the next four seasons, this would be Smith's show to run. Illinois found that out in a 33–20 loss to the Tigers before 61,876 fans at the Edwards Jones Dome in St. Louis.

Smith accounted for 290 yards of total offense in his first game for the Tigers—138 yards rushing and 152 passing. He was the first Tigers freshman quarterback to start an opener.

"If I told people I thought he was going to play like that, I'd be lying," Pinkel said after the game. "And I am not going to lie to you. I told many people behind the scenes that this guy is a remarkably talented athlete with remarkable poise. To play like that, first game, 18 years old, I'm just glad he's on my team. And I am glad he's a freshman."

If there was a defining moment for Brad Smith during his freshman season, it quite possibly came in a 31–24 loss to Oklahoma in Columbia in which Smith did everything but beat the powerful Sooners, who had to resort to a fake field goal for the deciding touchdown with 6:33 remaining in the game.

Smith accounted for 391 of Missouri's 449 yards (213 running and 178 yards) and three total touchdowns. Smith's 25-yard run put Missouri ahead 24–23 early in the fourth quarter.

"He's big time," said Oklahoma defensive back Matt McCoy. "He was just so mobile and makes so many plays. He's a great quarterback. And he is going to win a lot of games for that team."

"That was the game that put him on the map," Leon said. "He is just running up and down the field. It looked like he broke the free safety's ankle going into the end zone. He had the ability when he would get up next to the sideline, he would look like he was going out of bounds and then would cut against you and the guy would just be on his knees. He was deceptive. You didn't know how fast he really was. He probably only ran a 4.6."

In Smith's freshman season of 2002, Nebraska continued its mastery of Missouri with its 24th straight victory over the Tigers. The Huskers bottled up Smith and held him to 157 total offensive yards in Lincoln. That was less than half of the 332 yards of offense per game that Smith had been averaging. Nebraska sacked him four times.

"They had guys everywhere I went and did a great job of covering our receivers," Smith said after the game. "We needed to make adjustments on the field and we didn't do that... Nebraska brought pressure from everywhere and they did a great job of occupying the guys in the offensive line, which enabled them to bring guys from different directions."

Smith bounced back with a 275-yard passing outing in a 52–38 loss at Texas Tech. Missouri's defense just collapsed. Pinkel was exasperated.

"At the end of the game, I remember him [Pinkel] coming in and telling us he is not going to lose and he is not going to allow us to lose," Leon said. "He said we were the worst team he had ever coached. He was throwing stuff and almost tearful. I could see why he was frustrated. I will take part of the blame. The seniors never really stepped up. Brad had never been a real vocal guy and he was a just a freshman at that point in time."

The next week, Smith ran for 117 yards and passed for another 135 yards in a 36–12 rout of Kansas. Leon rushed for 104 yards and two touchdowns. The Tigers lost seven-point games to both Iowa State and Colorado (in overtime) by the same score, and beat Texas A&M in College Station, 33–27 (in double overtime).

A season-ending 38–0 loss to Kansas State kept the Tigers (5–7) from having a break-even season. But by the end of his freshman season, Smith had the most total offensive yards in a single season of any player in Missouri history with 3,362 yards, smashing Missouri quarterback Corby Jones's total of 2,545 in 1997.

By the time he was finished, he would have the top four offensive production seasons in Missouri history and become the leading career quarterback rusher in major-college history. His 1,029 yards rushing in 2002 were the most in history for a major-college freshman quarterback.

Missouri Tigers: Overtime Kings

Entering the 2008 season, Missouri and Northwestern had won more overtime games (eight) than any other teams in major-college football since the rule was instituted by the NCAA during the 1996 football season.

The Tigers and five other teams, entering the 2008 season, had been involved in the most overtime games of any teams in the Division I Football Bowl Subdivision—11. The Tigers have played in two three-overtime games and two double-overtime games and are 4–0 in those multiple-overtime contests.

The rundown:
1996–Missouri 35, Oklahoma State 28
1996–Missouri 49, Baylor 42 (3OT)
1997–Missouri 51, Oklahoma State 50 (2OT)
1997–Nebraska 45, Missouri 38
1999–Colorado 46, Missouri 39
2001–Missouri 41, Oklahoma State 38 (3OT)
2002–Colorado 42, Missouri 35
2002–Missouri 33, Texas A&M 27 (2OT)
2003–Missouri 41, Middle Tennessee 40
2004–Missouri 17, Iowa State 14
2005–Missouri 27, Iowa State 24

Missouri-Kansas Rivalry

The Missouri-Kansas football rivalry is the oldest west of the Mississippi River and the second longest in terms of games played among NCAA Football Bowl Subdivision teams

Through the 2007 season, the Tigers and Jayhawks will have met 116 times, ranking only behind Minnesota-Wisconsin, who have met 117 times.

The Missouri-Kansas rivalry dates to 1891, with only the 1918 game canceled because of an outbreak of influenza. The kindling for this fiery rivalry (it stands 54–53–9 in favor of Mississippi going into the 2008 season) can be traced back to the Civil War.

"I had no idea that rivalry existed until I got up there," said Leon, who is from Norman, Oklahoma. "I didn't even know the history behind it until I saw one of the History Channel shows. The Tigers were a gang and the Jayhawkers were in Lawrence. And Lawrence was a free town. And the Tigers came over to Lawrence and burned Lawrence to the ground. I didn't realize it until I got into it, how passionate the people were. How much they hated each other. I think that transferred over to the field.

"[The players] really did hate each other. How can I hurt this guy? What can I do to embarrass you? It was taunting non-stop. Even after the play was over, people getting up, sucker punching each other, clippings. It was the only game I ever played you just knew you were going to get into it. There was going to be a fight or a scuffle. You were going to do whatever you could to embarrass the other team. Each team thrived knocking somebody a step out of bounds. I just never heard so much profanity before in my life."

Nebraska Breakthrough: Independence Bowl Reward

Brad Smith's sophomore season (2003) brought the first victory over Nebraska since the 1978 season. The Tigers rallied for a 41–24 victory over the Huskers, prompting Missouri fans to tear down both sets of goal posts. On the sidelines were several Tiger players under former MU head coach Warren Powers, who defeated Nebraska in his very first season as the Tigers' head coach in 1978.

The Tigers won their first four games of the season and rose to a No. 23 ranking nationally before the 41–40 overtime victory over Middle Tennessee in the fourth game. The following week, Kansas upset Missouri, 35–14, heading into the showdown with 10th-ranked Nebraska in Columbia.

Smith had completed 140 straight passes without an interception before being intercepted in the first quarter by Nebraska. But he scored four touchdowns (three rushing, one receiving) as Missouri snapped a 20–game losing streak against Top 25–ranked teams in the Associated Press poll. The Tigers also posted their first victory over a Top Ten team at home since a 9–0 shut out of Arizona State in 1974.

"We blocked better," Pinkel said, referencing the KU game. "We were able to run draws and counter plays with Brad. We ran those same plays two weeks ago, but we didn't block very good…. I told Brad just to turn it loose. Don't be afraid to make bad throws. With his athleticism, if you're on eggshells, and you have to watch yourself on everything you do, then you can't use your athleticism."

The Nebraska victory served as Missouri's signature win of the season and included a fake field goal that turned into a touchdown and a throw-back pass to Brad Smith from Darius Outlaw, a former quarterback. But Smith's signature game of the season had to be a 62–31 victory over Texas Tech a few weeks later.

"That run he made along the sideline," Pinkel recalls of the Texas Tech game. "I just looked at the coaches next to me and shook my head. He is an amazing athlete and only a sophomore. He is going to get a lot better."

Smith rushed for 291 yards against Texas Tech, which was only 17 yards shy of tying an NCAA single-game record for rushing yards for a quarterback set by Stacey Robinson of Northern Illinois in 1990. Smith accounted for a school-record five rushing touchdowns against Texas Tech—10, 27, 2, 41, and 61 yards. Smith added 128 yards passing.

Missouri went to the Independence Bowl and fell to Arkansas, 27–14. But the Nebraska breakthrough victory stamped the season as a success, despite the fact that Missouri dropped games against Colorado and Kansas State late in the season and failed to win the Big 12 North title.

A Frustrating 2004 Season

Coming off the 8–5 season and bowl trip of 2003—the Tigers' first since 1998—optimism was high as Brad Smith entered his junior season. But questions arose regarding Smith's usage as a pocket passer instead of a runner. Further, poor nonconference scheduling on Missouri athletic director Mike Alden's part seemed to undercut the season.

"Brad Smith's ability was more about picking apart the defense," Leon said. "Then, when it was time, he would make a play. And that really hurt [Smith] when they tried to make him more of a pocket passer. After his first year, when you saw how successful he was, I don't know why they tried to change him with these long-developing pass routes."

During the 2004 season, Smith rushed for only 553 yards and posted his worst offensive total of his four seasons. Missouri wound up losing three home games, first to Oklahoma State and Kansas State, blowing 17–0 and 21–0 leads respectively in those games. The Tigers also lost to arch-rival Kansas, 31–14, in the 10th game of the season to assure a losing record (5–6). The 2004 season was tainted by an early loss to the Troy University Trojans from the Sun Belt Conference. Alden had scheduled a two-for-one series with the Trojans (two games in Columbia for one at Troy). Missouri would win the other two games in Columbia handily, but a 24–14 loss on ESPN2 to Troy was a Thursday night disaster for all to see.

Missouri jumped out to a 14–0 lead, but the Trojans scored the next 24 points on that humid evening in Troy, Alabama. The

Quarterback Brad Smith prepares to throw deep against Nebraska in an October 2004 game. The Tigers were less successful when Smith was used as a pocket passer rather than taking more advantage of his skill as a runner.

Tigers were guilty of three turnovers and suffered a blocked punt. They also saw a Trojan receiver throw a touchdown pass and an offensive lineman ramble 63 yards for a touchdown after a fumble by a teammate.

Troy finally beat a Big 12 Conference team in its seventh try. And Missouri stood 1–1 after two games.

"I think you earn respect for what you achieve," Pinkel said later. "And, as you're building a program [like Missouri is] and you lose a game like that, you lose respect. Guess what? You have to get it back. If you are an established program and it happens, you have been ranked nationally eight of the last 10 years, you lose a little respect. When you're a program building, like us, you lose a lot of it fast. You should lose it."

Missouri entered the Troy game nationally ranked and wouldn't return to the rankings during the 2004 season after the stunning upset. The Tigers finished 5–6.

Brad Smith's Last Hurrah

In 2005, Missouri qualified for a bowl for the second time in four years, with Smith leading the charge. The Tigers defeated Nebraska in Columbia for the second time in three years by exactly the same score, 41–24. Smith won National Player of the Week honors.

But 2005 would end like 2003, when Missouri contended for the Big 12 North title only to lose games down the stretch and fall out of contention. That's what happened, despite Smith becoming Missouri's all-time offense leader and the only quarterback in major-college history to pass for more than 8,000 yards and run for more than 4,000 in a career.

Further casting a pall on the 2005 season was the sudden death of linebacker Aaron O'Neal on July 12 after a voluntary conditioning workout. His death was caused by lymphocytic (viral) meningitis. The Tigers wore No. 25 patches throughout the 2005 season along with several other tributes to the 19–year-old from Creve Coeur, Missouri.

The Tigers could never convert Smith's talents into a league division title over a four-year period, despite the fact that perennial power Nebraska was going through a down period.

Missouri again lost an unexpected nonconference game in 2005, 45–35, to New Mexico when receiver Hank Baskett set career highs in three categories with 10 passes for 209 yards and three touchdowns.

Observers couldn't understand why Missouri's defense didn't start doubling Baskett and preventing the Lobos from continuously going over the top to the receiver. Smith did his part, with more than 400 yards total offense. But the defensive woes overshadowed everything else.

"We were so focused on [running back DonTrell Moore], we didn't think that [Baskett] was that great," said MU defender Xzavie Jackson.

Smith's senior season had an interesting twist—competition from freshman quarterback Chase Daniel. After Missouri defeated

Oklahoma State 38–31 in Stillwater, the Tigers returned home to face Iowa State in the sixth game of the season. Smith was hit in the head on a tackle by an Iowa State linebacker with just under nine minutes remaining in the game and Mizzou trailing, 24–14.

True freshman quarterback Chase Daniel from Carroll Senior High School in Southlake, Texas, came in and led drives of 75 yards (which ended in a field goal) and then 87 yards (which concluded with a touchdown pass to Sean Coffey) with 20 seconds remaining in the game. Daniel passed for 138 yards on the two drives to send the game into overtime, during which Missouri won with a field goal, 27–24.

The following week against Nebraska at Faurot Field, Missouri fans actually chanted to indicate that they wanted Daniel, not Smith, in the game. The score was tied 24–24 at halftime after Missouri had squandered a 24–10 lead.

"I think that in his career, [Smith] has had some adversity later on," Pinkel said. "He has found out the reality of playing quarterback. It's a little like being a coach. And he responded well. And the thing about him is he is a guy who battles back from adversity. That's Brad Smith."

Smith accounted for 480 yards of total offense against Nebraska. The Tigers blitzed the Huskers with a 17–0 second half and beat them in consecutive games in Columbia (2003 and 2005) for the first time since the Dan Devine era (1967 and 1969).

"It's hard to get motivated by that kind of stuff (fans' negative comments) because it wears off," Smith said. "And you just have to understand how people are."

But Missouri lost to Kansas, 13–3, for the third straight season with Smith, lost another North Division showdown against Colorado (41–12), and then fell to Kansas State (36–28) after blowing a lead in Manhattan. Only a 31–16 home win over Baylor kept Mizzou over .500

With Missouri teetering at 6–5, Smith saved the best for his final game, during which he led the greatest comeback in Missouri history in the Independence Bowl against South Carolina and Coach Steve Spurrier.

"We knew he was an excellent quarterback," Spurrier said. "We had him hemmed in the first half, but we weren't good enough to do it the whole game.... Twenty-one [to] nothing is no safe lead for us."

The Tigers fell behind 21–0 and were in danger of going down 28–0 when Marcus King intercepted a pass and returned it 99 yards for a touchdown. It was Mizzou's first interception returned for a touchdown in a bowl game since Dennis Poppe's 47-yard return for a score in the 1968 Gator Bowl victory against Alabama. The 99-yard interception return by King, who was the Independence Bowl Defensive MVP, is the longest in NCAA bowl game history for Football Bowl Subdivision teams.

Trailing 28–7, Missouri outscored South Carolina 31–3 over the last 30:20 of the game. Smith accounted for 432 yards (282 passing and 150 rushing) and four touchdowns on his way to receiving the Independence Offensive MVP honor.

Smith scored on runs of 31 and one yards in the final quarter. The latter touchdown run occurred with 2:01 remaining and pushed Mizzou ahead, 38–31. It also completed the comeback in Smith's final game as a Tiger.

"It wasn't anything magical," Smith told reporters after the game. "We just played within our system."

chapter 15
Chase Daniel Keeps it Going

"Chase Daniel never has stayed the same. He has never gotten worse. He has always gotten better. I think now he needs more consistency in the big game.... He has a picture of himself being successful at the highest level of college football."

—Todd Dodge

Going to the Spread Offense

Entering the 2006 season, there was already an aura surrounding sophomore quarterback Chase Daniel. He had come to Missouri from powerhouse Carroll Senior High School in suburban Dallas with a swagger.

And in 2005, as a true freshman, he had used that swagger in leading Missouri to a 27–24 overtime victory against Iowa State, playing in relief of injured senior Brad Smith. Daniel had more than swagger. He had the goods to become a top-flight quarterback in the Big 12 Conference.

"He was a backup and probably has had 25 reps in a Division I game," Missouri coach Gary Pinkel said. "In the Iowa State game, he goes in the fourth quarter. Drive, touchdown. Drive, field goal. We win the thing in overtime. I knew then, though he didn't start the rest of the football season. We had a football player there."

Despite Smith's presence as a senior, Missouri had gone to a spread offense in 2005 to eventually showcase Daniel.

"I am not surprised at all [he performed the way he did against Iowa State in 2005], because he went to Missouri without the red-shirt mentality," said Todd Dodge, Daniel's high-school coach and now the head coach at the University of North Texas. "I told Chase, 'You turn loose and compete and let the coaches decide.' He won the second-string job [behind Brad Smith].... Now, he is pretty special."

Dodge sold Missouri and Missouri sold Daniel on the fact they would run the same spread offense Carroll did. Daniel, as a starting high school quarterback, won 31 of 32 games his final two seasons and a state title as a senior.

"[The Missouri staff] had me speak at their spring clinic," Dodge said. "We did visit [about the offense]. It was while they were recruiting Chase. I sent them a DVD of Chase Daniel. And two weeks later, I was at their clinic."

While several Texas schools now wish they had recruited or shown greater interest in Daniel at the time (Texas and Texas A&M included), those schools had their sights set on other high-school

When Chase Daniel (shown passing during Missouri's 41–10 victory over Texas Tech in October 2007) took over as starting quarterback in the Tigers spread offense in 2006, they became one of the most dynamic offensive teams in the country.

quarterback prospects. Dodge had a longtime connection with Texas, obviously, as a former player there under Fred Akers. But he also had a connection with Missouri.

Dodge's grandfather, Don Swofford from Weatherford, Texas, lettered in football at Mizzou in 1924 and 1925. In his office at North Texas, Dodge has two pictures of his grandfather wearing his Missouri uniform.

Those mid-1920s Missouri teams also ran the spread. And the father of the modern era of Missouri football, Don Faurot, was a running back in that offense. In a way, Missouri football had come full cycle from the roaring 1920s.

Missouri coach Gary Pinkel tailor-made his offense for Daniel.

"Chase had 19 offers...none of the guys were on him like these guys were," Bill Daniel, Chase's father, said about Mizzou.

Other coaches say Pinkel was smart.

"[Pinkel] has a quarterback with a special talent and he knows how to handle a quarterback like that," said Toledo coach Tom Amstutz, Pinkel's former assistant. "Again, good coaches adjust to the personnel that they have."

The fact that Daniel was recruited by academic powerhouse Stanford is evidence that he is a special type of athlete who can make all the quick reads necessary in the no-huddle offense.

"Chase Daniel is a good player, the scheme is set up for him and he makes good decisions," said Western Michigan coach Bill Cubit, whose Broncos would later drop a 52–24 decision to Missouri in 2007. "He's a smart kid. When I was at Stanford, we recruited him. So I know a little bit about him. I don't think he came close [to going to Stanford]."

In his first game as a Missouri starter, against Murray State University in the 2006 season opener, Daniel passed for 320 yards and a Missouri-record five touchdowns and was on his way. The Tigers completed their second unbeaten nonconference record (4–0) in four years as the spread offense took hold in easy victories over Ole Miss and Ohio and a tough road victory at New Mexico. Missouri rose to a No. 24 ranking nationally before the 2006 Big 12 opener against Colorado.

Former Mississippi State, Texas A&M, and Pitt coach Jackie Sherrill is a big fan of Daniel. "What I like is his throwing motion, he doesn't take much time to throw it. He started off playing this system in the eighth grade." Sherrill also took note of the weapons Daniel had at his disposal, specifically Martin Rucker and Chase Coffman. "His tight ends are as good as any tight end tandem in the country."

Tigers' 6–0 Start in 2006: Best Since 1973

With a 28–13 victory over Colorado and a rousing 38–21 road victory over Texas Tech on Daniel's 20th birthday, Missouri moved to 6–0 for the first time in 33 years as Daniel flourished as a sophomore.

The Colorado victory was punctuated by Daniel's perform-ance, which included four touchdown passes against the Buffaloes in only his fifth game as a starter.

"He's got maturity, a lot of poise," Pinkel said. "That's why he moved up so fast. You coach poise and some guys can develop it, but he's just got it. He knows what he is doing. He's only played five games. Wait until he gets good. It'll be kind of fun to see what happens. I should preface that by saying this about Chase, he's got good players around him. He'd be the first one to tell you that."

In Daniel's first return to the Lone Star State the next week at Texas Tech, Missouri's defense turned in a first when the Tigers scored touchdowns on back-to-back plays in the second quarter. Xzavie Jackson intercepted a screen pass and returned it 17 yards for a touchdown. On the very next play, William Moore picked off a pass and took it back 22 yards to put Missouri ahead, 24–0. Daniel had 173 yards passing and a touchdown.

Texas Tech also committed two fumbles and wound up getting blown out by the Tigers, 38–21. That victory pushed Missouri to 6–0 overall and 2–0 in the Big 12 going into a game at College Station, in which the Tigers had their chances, but fell, 25–19.

"I told him when he played at College Station, 'Don't look up in the stands,'" Dodge recalled advising Daniel. "It will look like an earthquake [with the fans swaying]. He played well before 80,000 screaming Aggies. He got confidence."

The following week, Missouri ended a 13-year losing streak against Kansas State (41–21), then recorded its only home loss of the season to Oklahoma (26–10), before losing at Nebraska (34–20). But Daniel attempted to lead Missouri back against the Huskers in Lincoln.

Daniel talked to the team on the sideline to try and coax them back into the game. "Do you see how easy that was?" he said. "We can do that one play at a time."

Former University of Houston star quarterback Andre Ware was a color analyst on the Missouri-Nebraska game in Lincoln. "They are just playing into Nebraska's hands with the little runs and screens," he told fans. "They need to attack them downfield....

They need to line the tight end up at the normal position or the slot position."

Nevertheless, Daniel (with 244 yards) went from fifth to first in a single-season passing at Missouri (2,531 yards in 10 games), passing Jeff Handy's mark of 2,463 yards in 1992. And the following week against Iowa State, Daniel actually scored from the 1-yard line on fourth down with 26 seconds remaining, but it was disallowed by officials. Later the Big 12 reviewed the play and announced the officials had erred on the holding call and the touchdown should have counted. Missouri should have won.

"I was just shocked," Daniel said after Missouri's 21–16 loss. "No offense to them, but they never should have beaten us. I'm not used to losing and it's hard.... We shouldn't have been in this position in the first place."

Daniel passed Kansas silly the final game of the regular season, amassing 356 yards and four touchdowns through the air in a 42–17 victory. Tight end Chase Coffman caught two of the passes for touchdowns. Jared Perry snared a 74-yard pass from Daniel, which was Missouri's longest pass play in 17 years.

The Tigers (8–4) played Oregon State in the Sun Bowl, the third bowl game in four seasons under Pinkel. The Beavers trailed Missouri by 14 points with 12:08 remaining, but Oregon State roared back for two touchdowns, the final one with 22.1 seconds remaining, to narrow the score to 38–37. The game appeared to be headed for overtime, but Oregon State converted a surprise two-point conversion run up the middle to beat Mizzou, 39–38, despite 330 yards passing by Daniel.

"I think he can be fabulous the next two years," Dodge said. "Chase Daniel never has stayed the same. He has never gotten worse. He has always gotten better. I think now he needs more consistency in the big game. He has done some real good things. He had a great game at Texas Tech last year, but some of the big games he needs to be a more consistent player and go to the next step. He has a picture of himself being successful at the highest level of college football."

Despite the loss to Oregon State, Missouri had great reason to look forward to the 2007 season. Daniel would be back, along with tight ends Coffman and Rucker. Temple would return as well. The offensive line would be strong. A bevy of other receivers would be at Daniel's disposal—Tommy Saunders, Will Franklin, Jeremy Maclin, Jared Perry, and Danario Alexander—heading into his junior season.

And there were some other areas that might have been overlooked as the Tigers prepared themselves to climb the ladder into the Top 5 college football teams in 2007.

The Tigers were the only club in the Big 12 to be ranked in the Top 3 in the league in both total offense and defense. Eleven different Mizzou defenders had sacks. The Tigers were also 33rd nationally in scoring defense (19.5 points allowed a game), which was fourth-best in the Big 12.

Of course, the offense was dazzling in 2006. Missouri was eighth in the country in total offense and 10th in passing. Fifteen different players caught passes in 2006. Seven players had 14 or more catches, and six had 25 or more. Missouri registered 16 rushing touchdowns by six different players.

"There are no negative influences on this team," said Bill Daniel, father of Chase, during an alumni gathering in the spring of 2007. "There are a lot of leaders on this team. Tony Temple and the offensive line are very important to us. I have had guys come up to me and say, 'Chase got sacked. It was my fault. I will never do it again.'"

Missouri also had one of the top kickers in Big 12 returning for his junior season in 2007. As a sophomore, Jeff Wolfert, the former Mizzou diver, connected on 18 of 20 field goal attempts and was a perfect 45–45 on extra point attempts.

The Sun Bowl collapse raised questions in the off-season about Missouri's running game and the sometimes-dangerous use of Daniel as a runner, risking injury. Missouri, playing without a fullback and often failing to sustain long drives with leads, had to run Daniel or Tony Temple or just keep passing, which stopped the clock.

Missouri coaches were somewhat sensitive when asked about the absence of a fullback for short-yardage situations near the goal line and use in a time-consuming ground game, which might protect leads in 2007.

"You have to pick what you want to do," said Bruce Walker, Missouri's assistant offensive line and tight ends coach. "Missouri had a fullback for a long time [and didn't win]. We have a guy who is special. I have been 20 years coaching football and I have seen some really good quarterbacks. To have him line up in the I-formation with a fullback makes no sense to me."

During the 2006 season, Daniel's health was in question at times, because of the punishment he absorbed during games. He often had to run the ball near the goal line because MU's other backs, including Tony Temple, were ineffective in the red zone. At 6', 225 pounds, Daniel is stocky and a tough player to bring down with just a casual arm tackle. His darting-and-dashing ability is patterned after his idol, Green Bay Packers star Brett Favre.

"They have a tremendous young player," said former OU assistant coach and Missouri player Merv Johnson, the Sooners' radio analyst. "[Brad]Smith would try and slide or squirm in between, but this guy tries to go right through them.... You just can't ask him to do everything."

Daniel started sliding more in 2007, and Missouri did develop a better running game. The Tigers would also insert tight end Martin Rucker into the shotgun and run him near the goal line at times. When teams such as Texas Tech and Arkansas tried to press the receivers with man coverage all over the field, Missouri allowed its running backs to carry the day. They were able to hit the open seams of the defense.

chapter 16
BCS Dreams...
and Nightmares

"I told my wife I'd like this to be my last job.... I know a lot of friends called me up and told me I was crazy when I took this job.... Everything has changed. The dynamics have changed. We continue to work hard, and we continue to build."

—Gary Pinkel

Seasons to Remember for Maclin, Daniel

Missouri was unranked at the start of the 2007 season, but there was a bundle of talent in Columbia, including Jeremy Maclin, a freshman redshirt from Kirkwood, Missouri, a suburb of St. Louis. He had originally committed to Oklahoma, but when pressed by the Sooners staff to make a firm commitment, Maclin backed off. Missouri was the lucky school to reel in the game-breaker.

"He grew up an hour and a half from [Columbia]," Pinkel said. "He committed early to OU. We are very fortunate he changed his mind. We all knew he would be an impact player. He has had a huge impact. I expected he would be a great player, but I didn't know he would play at this level his first season. His maturity allows him to play as this level."

Maclin suffered a knee injury that required surgery in the summer before his freshman year. He wound up missing the entire 2006 season.

"I think it made him more motivated," Daniel said. "That year off football put a chip on his shoulder. I think he thought 'I have to get back to help this team as quick as I can.'"

Maclin was ready for Missouri's 2007 opener in St. Louis against Illinois and added a new dimension to the Tigers' special teams as well as their offense.

"He goes into the Illinois game, at his home in St. Louis, in the dome, has not played a college football game yet, and he goes out and has the game he had," Pinkel said.

"When we played in the Illinois game and Jeremy Maclin did as well as he did, he was the 'X' factor, that thing we needed to go ahead and have a great season," Missouri tight end Martin Rucker said of a 40–34 Missouri victory over Illinois.

With Missouri leading 23–13 in the third quarter, Maclin caught his first touchdown pass, a 25-yarder from Daniel. Less than four minutes later, Maclin returned a punt 66 yards for a touchdown and a 37–13 Missouri lead. By the end of the game, Maclin had 227 all-purpose yards and provided two crucial scores.

"It gave me faith and confidence all over again," Maclin said of coming back from a serious injury. "I did that in front of my home crowd, and it just made me enjoy football again. All my doubts went out the window."

It was a just a glimpse of things to come the rest of the 2007 season.

Maclin registered an NCAA freshman record with more than 2,776 all-purpose yards (receiving, rushing, punt, and kickoff returns). That total ranks as the fifth best of all time by any player in NCAA Football Bowl Subdivision history. He was the only player in 2007 in the division to have touchdowns in all four categories of receiving (nine), rushing (four), punt return (two), and kick return (one). Maclin had more than 200 yards in all-purpose yards in seven games and more than 300 yards once, with 360 yards and three touchdowns in a 49–32 victory over Kansas State in the 11th game of the season.

"The good news about him is he will keep getting better and better," Pinkel said of Maclin. "He can get a lot better. Fundamentally, he can get better. He can play smarter, through experience and the little things it takes to be a great receiver, especially with the complexity of offenses and defenses now. He'll continue to improve and work hard. I think he has a chance to be a great player."

Missouri Makes Breakthrough

In 2006, the Tigers lost at Texas A&M, 25–19, and would drop four of their last six regular-season games to fall out of contention for the Big 12 North Division title. In 2007, for a second straight season, Missouri was undefeated going into mid-October. But this season would be different after a hiccup at OU.

ESPN's "GameDay" with Kirk Herbstreit, Lee Corso, and Chris Fowler, were present outside Owen Field in the match-up between the two nationally ranked teams, No. 6 Oklahoma and No. 11 Missouri on Oct. 13.

The Tigers had swept past their first five opponents. After beating Illinois, the Tigers won at Ole Miss, 38–25. They then took consecutive home games against Western Michigan, 52–24, and Illinois State, 38–17. They then thumped No. 24 Nebraska, 41–6, in the Big 12 opener before 70,049 fans in the Gold Rush game. Much to the chagrin of Husker fans, Missouri scored on a fake field goal in the fourth quarter. Nebraska's season of misery was just beginning.

In the fifth game, Missouri actually led Oklahoma, 24–23, early in the fourth quarter. The Tigers were seeking to beat both OU and Nebraska in the same season for the first time since 1969, the last time they had played in a New Year's Day game. Mizzou's strong safety Cornelius "Pig" Brown couldn't hang on to a pass thrown by OU's freshman quarterback Sam Bradford in the end zone early in the fourth quarter. OU eventually scored to take a 29–24 lead before a two-point conversion pass failed.

Then came Missouri's misplay of the game.

Daniel attempted a handoff to Maclin, but the two didn't connect. The ball wound up on the turf. OU's alert linebacker Curtis Lofton picked up the fumble and went 12 yards for a touchdown. After a missed kick (PAT), OU led by 11 with 11:40 remaining in the game.

"That was a coaching error," Pinkel said of the fumble, explaining that neither player was to blame because the play was miscommunicated from the sideline. "It was a huge play. It was not only a turnover, but points."

The Tigers still had not beaten Oklahoma in Norman since the 1966 season (10–7), a period of 41 years. But the Tigers actually out-gained the Sooners in total yards, 418–384, without starting running back Tony Temple, who was out with a sprained right ankle that he suffered the previous week in the game against Nebraska.

"Even though we lost to Oklahoma, how well we played was special to us," Daniel said. "That was a turning point. After we watched the film, we thought we gave the ballgame away in the fourth quarter. We thought, 'Hey, we can play with anybody in the nation if we can cut down on our mistakes.'"

Through the first six games of Missouri's 5–1 season, Daniel had thrown 16 touchdowns and passed for 359 (Illinois), 330 (Ole Miss), 328 (Western Michigan), 294 (Illinois State), 401 (Nebraska), and 361 yards (Oklahoma). As Todd Dodge had predicted, Daniel would get better as a junior.

"A player with humility always gets better, because they know they haven't arrived," Pinkel said. "He's been a tremendous leader. He's also a great visual aid for any quarterback coming in to watch what this guy does. He's also a great visual aid for those players around for the right way to lead. He's probably the best in the toughest parts of the game."

In the seventh game of the season, Missouri had to bounce back from the OU loss without Temple, who was still sidelined with his bum ankle. So No. 22 Texas Tech, which also plays the spread offense, tried to press the Tigers receivers and take away the MU passing game and test the team's backup tailbacks.

Neither Daniel nor the Mizzou coaching staff would force the issue, throwing the ball against this stacked defense. Daniel had regular-season lows of 210 passing yards on only 19 attempts as the MU running game took hold. The Tigers ran it up the gut behind their big offensive line. Junior tailback Jimmy Jackson (59 yards and three touchdowns) and freshman Derrick Washington (66 yards) made the Red Raiders pay. The Tiger defense also stepped up in a rousing 41–10 victory. Going into the game, the Red Raiders had the nation's top offense. But the opportunistic and harassing Tigers defense intercepted Texas Tech quarterback Graham Harrell four times.

After posting a 6–1 record with the victory over Texas Tech, Missouri faced one of those dangerous "sandwich games" against Iowa State, a team that had struggled most of the season. The week before, Iowa State had played Oklahoma to within 17–7 before losing. On the way to a 3–9 season, Iowa State surprised both Kansas State and Colorado—but not Missouri. The Tigers prevailed, 42–28.

The Tigers also welcomed back Temple for the first time since early November. He gained 40 yards on a modest eight carries and scored a touchdown. The downer for the Tigers was the loss for the season of 5'11", 205-pound senior safety Pig Brown to a ruptured Achilles tendon suffered in the fourth quarter against the Cyclones after making 10 tackles in the game.

MU Defense Solidifies

Brown, from Adel, Georgia, by way of Reedley College in Reedley, California, had been an inspirational player as well as a key performer during the 2007 season. He was named Big 12 Defensive Player of the Week twice (Illinois and Texas Tech) and Bronko Nagurski National Defensive Player of the Week once (Illinois).

Brown recovered two fumbles against Illinois in the season opener. One of those fumbles he recovered in the end zone as Illinois was about to score. Brown returned it 100 yards (tying an NCAA record) and turned a 7–6 lead into a 13–6 advantage. He also made an interception at the 1-yard line in the final minute of a 40–34 MU victory.

Was this an ominous sign that the Tigers would collapse? In 2006, Missouri, in its eighth game—a 41–21 victory over Kansas State—lost standout defensive end Brian Smith for the season. He was possibly on his way to a Big 12 sack record but suffered a season-ending fractured right hip. Standing 7–1 with a chance at the Big 12 North title, the 2006 Tigers then lost three of their last four regular-season games. They never did play with the same defensive fire after Smith was out of the lineup.

But in 2007, 6'1", 220-pound junior free safety William Moore stepped up in the secondary and made up for Brown's absence. In four of the last five regular-season games, he intercepted a pass and raised his regular-season total to seven, which ranked third in the nation before the Cotton Bowl. He then topped his regular season off by being named the Cotton Bowl's Most Outstanding Defensive Player in the Tigers' 38–7 victory over Arkansas.

"Before I went out there [the week after Brown's injury], I said, 'I have to step [up with] the loss of Pig Brown,'" Moore said. "I knew

I had to take on more of the leadership role. [Pig] stood up before the game [against Colorado on November 3] and told the defense that we could play without him. He got a little emotional and we all got a little emotional."

Moreover, the entire Tigers defense was much better in the eight Big 12 Conference regular-season games—when, presumably, the competition was tougher—than it was in the first four games of the season against nonconference competition, i,e., Illinois, Mississippi, Western Michigan, and Illinois State.

The Tigers went from 11th in the league (after the first four nonconference games) to first in the league in total defense (434.5 yards a game to 353.9) in league games only, from ninth to second in rushing defense (158.8 yards a game to 93.0), from 10th to second in pass efficiency defense (123.3 to 117.7), from eighth to third in scoring defense (25.0 to 22.6 points allowed a game), and from 11th to third in pass defense (275.8 to 260.9 yards allowed a game). And Brown missed the final four regular-season games in November against Colorado, Texas A&M, Kansas State, and Kansas. MU linebacker Sean Witherspoon wrote "PIG" in his eye black at the Cotton Bowl.

"[Brown] was the driving force," said another senior, MU nose tackle Lorenzo Williams. "He wouldn't let us stop. He wouldn't let us quit.... He refused to let us go down when he went down. That's a great credit to him... I was thinking after he got hurt, I am going to have go in there and lead by myself.... Our defense responded well when he went down. Will Moore definitely stepped up and did a great job the rest of the year."

In the Cotton Bowl game, Moore was at his best when he notched 13 tackles, forced a fumble, and returned an interception for a touchdown. He was part of the Mizzou defense that hounded Darren McFadden, who finished with just 105 yards on 21 carries. He also was a part of crushing tackle that forced a McFadden fumble.

"Lorenzo came up to me, he was [saying], 'I need a takeaway. I need an interception from you,'" Moore said of the conversation before his big pick in the third quarter. "I told him, 'If you all would let the quarterback throw the ball."

"They swarm the ball extremely well," said Arkansas's interim head coach, Reggie Herring. "They're a very physical defense.... At the end of the day, does a team play fast and play hard consistently for four quarters? That's the question I ask, and that's what they do."

"Chase-ing" Big November Victories

November is the time when championships are won. And Missouri had not won a league championship of any kind in football since 1969. When Pinkel met with his seniors prior to the 2007 season, he said they discussed winning big games down the stretch. This hadn't happened when the Tigers had dropped pivotal games in 2005 and 2006 down the stretch.

"We discussed the things you had to do to win at a higher level," Pinkel said. "Everyone wants to win at a higher level, but how are you going to do it? That's being better at turnover margin, win games on the road, win games in November...and keep winning to get to the Big 12 [championship game]. We overcame a lot of hurdles. There were a lot of things thrown in front of this football team. We made tremendous strides."

Missouri's game at Colorado on November 3 was one of those hurdles. The Tigers had not won in Boulder since 1997 and had lost four straight there. They not only won there, they won resoundingly, notching a 55–10 victory and scoring the most points CU had given up at home since a 59–20 loss to Missouri in 1983. Junior tight end Chase Coffman caught three touchdown passes from Daniel and even hurdled a Colorado defender into the end zone. He became MU's career touchdown reception leader.

"I get tired of people going at my knees," said Coffman after the game. "So I jumped over them today and it worked. I didn't run track

Chase Coffman—shown pulling in a pass during the 2008 Cotton Bowl—and Martin Rucker were two of the nation's top tight ends in 2007, and reliable targets for Chase Daniel.

in high school or anything. My dad [Paul] used to play and I have seen videos of him doing that, so I thought I would give it a try."

Daniel threw five touchdown passes against Colorado, matching his school record in two previous games. His 421 yards passing were a career high against a Colorado team that had beaten eventual Big 12 champion Oklahoma on the same field,

27–24, and given much-improved Kansas all it wanted before losing 19-14.

"He's a good quarterback," Colorado linebacker Jordon Dizon said of Daniel. "He makes plays with his arm and his feet. He's a two-dimensional quarterback, and that's tough to defend. If you cover the pass, he runs the ball. And if you defend against his scrambling abilities, he'll beat you with the pass."

Against Colorado, Daniel had 445 yards of total offense, his second highest total of the season behind his career-high 473 yards (401 passing and 72 rushing) in the earlier victory over Nebraska.

"Chase Daniel started this in high school," Pinkel said. "The guy won state championships. He is a winner and a tenacious competitor. He is a battlefield commander.... I think he is more in charge of everything that is going on [as opposed to 2006]. I think that he has a lot more suggestions now. He sees more of the field. On Mondays, when we are game-planning, he is spending a lot of time sitting there game-planning with all the coaches. Sometimes, with his opinions, we will make fun of him. But most of the time he gives opinions that are good. He's a student of the game and obviously a bright guy."

With 367 yards total offense and a season-best 189.91 efficiency rating in a 40–26 victory over Texas A&M in Game 10, Daniel helped Missouri move to 9–1 for the first time since 1969. Daniel also jumped into the Heisman Trophy talk.

After the victory over Texas A&M, Missouri rose to a No. 6 ranking in the Associated Press poll and a highest-ever No. 5 ranking in the Bowl Championship Series standings. But there was another hurdle: winning at Kansas State in Week 11. The Tigers had not won in Manhattan since 1989 and had dropped eight straight games to the Wildcats on their home field.

A win over the Wildcats would set up a North Division championship game against unbeaten Kansas in the final game of the regular season on a neutral field in Kansas City, Missouri, at Arrowhead Stadium. The Tigers and Kansas had signed a two-year agreement to move KU's home game in 2007 and Missouri's home game in 2008 to the NFL stadium. The dream game would have legs after the Tigers bounced Kansas State, 49–32.

Against Kansas State, Daniel threw for four touchdowns, including two to Maclin, who scored the Tigers' first two touchdowns. The first was on an eight-yard pass after an interception by Moore early in the game. Maclin then went 99 yards with Missouri's first kickoff return for a touchdown since Ricky Doby had scored on a reverse against Oklahoma State in 1982.

Maclin's third touchdown was a 44-yard pass from Daniel in the third quarter on the way to a Missouri-record 360 all-purpose yards. With the performance against the Wildcats, Maclin solidified his position as one of two consensus All-Americans on the 2007 Missouri team (along with tight end Martin Rucker). It was the first time in the history of the school that two players were so named in the same season.

"Maclin is playing at an unbelievable level right now," Daniel said before the KU game. "He prepares as well as anyone I have met in football. He is fast and has all the intangibles.... There are not many people in college football who change a game on one play like he can."

Tight Ends, Big Offensive Line Open it Up for Daniel

Missouri's two-headed tight end monster combination of the 6'6", 245-pound Coffman and 6'6", 255-pound senior Martin Rucker was simply too much for teams to handle during the 2007 season. Rucker stayed for his senior season and it paid off as he became a consensus first-team All-American. He led the nation's tight ends with 84 receptions for 834 yards and eight touchdowns in 2007. Rucker finished at Mizzou as the career leader in receptions with 203.

"He's making plays, breaking tackles, and he's also doing a great job leading," Pinkel said during the 2007 season. "It's very encouraging when one of your best players from a year ago has upped his game to a level that maybe we didn't think he could be at."

Coffman, who will return for his senior season in 2008, ranked third in Missouri career receptions with 157 at the end of the 2007 season and is already the MU career leader in touchdown receptions with 20.

Both Rucker and Coffman have professional football ties. Coffman's father, Paul, was a standout tight end at Kansas State and then played for the Green Bay Packers (1978–85), Kansas City Chiefs (1986–87), and the Minnesota Vikings (1988). Rucker's brother, Mike, was an end at Nebraska (1995–98) and still plays for the Carolina Panthers.

"It is definitely a luxury," Daniel said of having the two tight ends who should have NFL careers. "Many teams are hard pressed to have one talented tight end. And we have two…. We like to distribute the ball. It is the hardest part of my job, but I also have the best job in America. I am getting great protection from my offensive line and throwing to my play-makers."

Missouri's offensive line was solid in 2007 as well, allowing Daniel plenty of time to find his bevy of receivers and tight ends. The five starting linemen for Mizzou were all from small Missouri towns, some just dots on the map: senior left tackle Tyler Luellen and junior left guard Ryan Madison were from Bethany (population: 3,082), senior center Adam Spieker was from Webb City (population: 10,982), sophomore right guard Kurtis Gregory was from Blackburn (population: 276), and junior right tackle Colin Brown was from Braymer (population: 958).

"Ours should [get more recognition]," Daniel said of his offensive line. "They've been playing at a very high level the whole year. I think it is one thing that has been overlooked. I try to tell people. But week in and week out, they're playing at a very high level."

In the showdown with unbeaten and No. 2-ranked Kansas (11–0), the Tigers' offensive line and Daniel were dominant as Mizzou's offense produced early. The third-ranked Tigers (10–1) jumped out to a 14–0 halftime lead and dominated the Jayhawks, 36-28, in becoming the only team in the NCAA Football Bowl Subdivsion to score 30 or more points in all 12 regular-season games during the 2007 season.

Daniel knew the importance of the KU game. He had had a big game the previous season when Missouri solidified its bowl position and basically knocked KU out of a bowl game with a 42–17 victory in Columbia.

"I was up visiting Columbia on my unofficial visit—me and [MU quarterbacks coach David] Yost were at a creamery getting ice cream," Daniel said. "Someone said, 'Beat KU all four years, no matter what, we will love you.'"

With a crowd of 80,537 (evenly divided between MU and KU fans) watching in the 116th game in the bitter border rivalry, Daniel completed 40 of 49 passes for 361 yards, three touchdowns, and no interceptions. Daniel's one-yard touchdown pass to Rucker gave MU a 7–0 lead in the first quarter. His 11-yard pass to Danario Alexander in the second quarter pushed the Tigers ahead, 14–0, capping a 98-yard drive. And Jimmy Jackson's one-yard run in the third quarter made it 21–0 MU.

Kansas, frustrated in the first half when Scott Webb missed two field goals and quarterback Todd Reesing was intercepted near the end zone by MU's William Moore, scored its first touchdown midway through the third quarter. But the Tigers answered with Daniel's third touchdown pass (a three-yarder to Derrick Washington) that pushed the lead back to 28–7. While KU was in rally mode, Missouri's lead was too substantial for the Jayhawks to overcome. Reesing was sacked in the end zone for a safety by MU's Lorenzo Williams with 12 seconds remaining.

"The environment (at the MU-KU game) was one of the best I have been around in 30 years of coaching," Pinkel said.

Missouri's victory, combined with top-ranked LSU's 50–48 triple overtime loss to Arkansas the previous day, vaulted the Tigers to the No. 1 ranking in the Associated Press poll for only the second time in school history. The previous No. 1 ranking came in the 1960 season before the Tigers played KU in the final game of the regular season. The victory also moved MU into the No. 2 position in the Bowl Championship Series standings.

"This is the dream that [assistant coach Andy] Hill and Coach Pinkel were talking about in my living room," Rucker said of playing for a Big 12 title and a place in the national title game. "We would be the class to do it, if it didn't happen before."

With a victory over Oklahoma, Missouri could vault into the BCS 1–2 game in New Orleans on January 7.

Losing to Oklahoma Again; BCS Snub

Missouri, playing in its first Big 12 Championship game, needed to reverse two losses to the Sooners in the previous 14 months. In addition to the earlier defeat to OU in the 2007 season, Missouri had lost to OU in Columbia, 26–10, during the 2006 season. In those first two games, Daniel had six turnovers.

"In the other game [in 2007 in Norman], we shot ourselves in the foot," Rucker noted of the fourth quarter fumble that resulted in an OU touchdown. "We didn't give ourselves a chance to win."

But OU had a formula to stop MU/Daniel.

"We tried not to just let him see one thing [defensively]," Oklahoma coach Bob Stoops said of the first MU game in 2007 when the Sooners scored 18 straight points in the fourth quarter to win. "We wanted him to figure out what he was seeing after he got the ball snapped.... We just mixed up what we were doing. We had three-five blitzes, three-five coverages. We did an excellent job of changing and blitzing."

The Sooners did the same thing in the rematch. Daniel never did get into a real rhythm in the game at the Alamodome.

Missouri was without its leading rusher, Tony Temple, in the first game in Norman but was within easy striking distance in the fourth quarter. Thus, there was a confidence factor at MU. The Tigers would have Temple for the rematch, but would be missing tight end Chase Coffman. Coffman initially was hurt in the first Oklahoma game and he would miss this one entirely with an ankle injury suffered in the victory over KU.

Missouri held its own in the first half of the championship game and played the Sooners to a 14–14 tie. With West

Virginia losing to Pittsburgh, the Tigers would play Ohio State for the national title if they could beat OU in the final 30 minutes.

But Missouri could only manage a field goal in the second half as the Sooners, behind freshman quarterback Sam Bradford, scored 24 points to take a 38–17 victory. The Tigers were without both Coffman and Alexander in the second half after Alexander suffered a knee injury late in the first half.

The absence of Coffman was apparent in the first half when Mizzou drove deep into OU territory and twice had to settle for field goals. And in the second half, Daniel was intercepted by linebacker Curtis Lofton to set up a touchdown that put OU up, 28–14. Ballgame.

Mizzou's junior kicker, Jeff Wolfert, finished off a perfect year against Big 12 teams—41-for-41 in extra points and 15-of-15 in field goals, including the Big 12 title game against OU in which he kicked three field goals.

At the end of the regular season, Daniel would rank among the top players in the country in nearly every statistical category for quarterbacks and finished fourth in the Heisman Trophy balloting behind the winner, Florida quarterback Tim Tebow, Arkansas running back Darren McFadden and Hawaii quarterback Colt Brennan. Missouri's only other Heisman Trophy finalist in history was Paul Christman, who finished third in 1939.

Daniel was also one of three finalists for the Davey O'Brien Award (national quarterback award, won by Tebow) and became Mizzou's first Big 12 Offensive Player of the Year winner. His 2007 season included school single-season records for Missouri passing yards, touchdown passes, and total offense.

"I am impressed with how he gets rid of the ball," said Arkansas former defensive coordinator Louis Campbell before the Razorbacks met the Tigers in the Cotton Bowl. "He is going to get rid of the ball before [the defense] gets to him. I'm also impressed with how he can pull the ball down and run it. He can make you miss and turn the corner…. It looks like you have him, then all of a sudden he has great escape ability."

Given Missouri's scoring power and Daniel's celebrity, it might have been generally assumed MU would be going to one of the five BCS bowls. Oklahoma, as Big 12 champion, automatically went to the Fiesta Bowl. But since MU beat KU, would the nod go to the Tigers for the at-large selection the league was expected to get?

Daniel and the rest of the Tigers were initially disappointed that Missouri was not selected for the Bowl Championship Series. The Orange Bowl picked the 11–1 Jayhawks over the Tigers (11–2), fresh off the 38–17 loss to OU, to play Virginia Tech, despite the fact the Tigers, ranked No. 6 in the BCS standings, had beaten the Jayhawks in a head-to-head meeting. To further add to that disappointment, Illinois, another team the Tigers beat during the regular season, went to the BCS Rose Bowl because of its Big Ten affiliation. Missouri was the only team to beat two 2007 BCS Bowl teams.

"We beat them, but we lost [to Oklahoma] at the wrong time," Daniel said at the time. "We cannot hold our heads down."

Instead of cursing their luck, the Tigers embraced their trip to Dallas, which was actually Daniel's hometown. He played high school football at nearby Carroll Senior High School. He was excited. And the rest of the Tigers became excited to play in Missouri's first New Year's Day game since losing to Penn State, 10–3, on January 1, 1970.

"Initially, we were upset for about a couple of days after we heard," Rucker said. "But we knew the Cotton Bowl was a great bowl. We felt that we deserved, that we had earned a BCS game. That's all that was. The Cotton Bowl is a great bowl and we were honored to play in it."

Pinkel stressed the positives of playing in a New Year's Day bowl in Texas. Missouri had 18 players on its Cotton Bowl roster from the Lone Star State, including Alexander, who was out with a knee injury.

"When I found out we were going to the Cotton Bowl, the very prestigious bowl in Dallas, one of our main recruiting areas in the whole state of Texas [I was happy], " Pinkel said. "[The high school coaches in Dallas] got a chance to see us coach and interact with our players. You can talk about that at clinics. You can meet our assistant coaches who recruit down here or myself, but [you can't see] how we interact, how we teach, how we coach.... I think that's a real plus for us."

Pinkel's Personality Transformation

Shortly before Christmas 2007, Missouri rewarded Pinkel with a contract extension and raise. With Missouri on the way to notching a record number of victories in one season at MU (12), the school's first No. 1 ranking since 1960, and first football title (North Division crown) of any kind since 1969, Pinkel was given a one-year extension through the 2012 season. He was awarded a $550,000 annual raise, which moved his salary up to $1.85 million a year.

Rumors had surfaced in December that Michigan might come after Pinkel. But Pinkel's new contract ended any speculation that he would leave Missouri any time soon. At Missouri since the 2001 season, Pinkel finished the 2007 season with a 49–37 overall record at MU and with prospects for a bright 2008 season and several strong ones after that.

"Everybody has talked about Missouri forever," a much more relaxed Pinkel said during Cotton Bowl week. "Why can't Missouri win? Only Division I school in the state of Missouri...St. Louis and Kansas City, all those things. I told my wife I'd like this to be my last job.

"[Before I took the job] I thought Missouri was a place where, if they did the right things and not fire coaches every four years, you could build at Missouri," Pinkel said. "I know a lot of friends called me up and told me I was crazy when I took this job, in a little bit more polite way than that.... We haven't arrived [yet].... We lost to Oklahoma in the championship game. But as you well know, our facilities are as nice as there are in the country. Everything has changed. The dynamics have changed. We continue to work hard, and we continue to build."

Missouri players said Pinkel, the complete coach, may have arrived in 2007. He mellowed that season, without losing his edge for winning.

"It's hard to explain," said Lorenzo Williams. "He is completely a different guy. He is the same guy. His values and leadership have not changed at all. But he is definitely now a personable coach.

"He used to be peanut butter and now he's kind of like jelly," Williams added. "Peanut butter's real thick. He used to not be real approachable. But he took that upon himself to have better relationships with his players and to become a better coach."

The transformation really began, Pinkel said, after the death of Missouri Tiger Aaron O'Neal, a redshirt freshman linebacker, on July 12, 2005. O'Neal, from Parkway North High School in St. Louis, passed away after a voluntary workout with teammates in Columbia.

"I think I have lightened up," Pinkel said during Cotton Bowl week. "I let my guard down a lot. And I did that after the Aaron O'Neal tragedy.... I am older now. I'm a little more mature. You get to be 55 and eventually you mature. My big thing was I wanted to be around my players and to get to know them better. I still want to maintain the discipline for our program...but I've enjoyed coaching as much as I've ever enjoyed coaching."

Daniel said he had found Pinkel more approachable. Once, early in the 2007 season, Daniel mustered up the courage to ask Pinkel again about wearing a baseball cap on the sidelines as he did at Carroll.

"I went by his office," Daniel said. "He was whistling. I thought, I will ask it one more time. I thought, If I don't get it this time, I will not ask one more time. Luckily he was in a pretty good mood."

Wish granted.

Cotton Bowl Buildup, Then Glory

Arkansas players talked trash about Missouri's tight ends Coffman and Rucker before the Cotton Bowl. And the two big tight ends caught only four balls between them for a total of 27 yards in Missouri's lopsided 38–7 victory. But the Razorbacks loaded up to stop Daniel's passing and were exposed by the runs of senior tailback Tony Temple, who set two Cotton Bowl records in rushing for 281 yards and four touchdowns.

Arkansas strong safety Matt Hewitt and linebacker Weston Dacus questioned how good Missouri's tight ends were. Hewitt said Missouri was in for a "rude awakening" and bragging about the Southeastern Conference, of which the Razorbacks are a part. Arkansas interim head coach Reggie Herring said those players "got put in the corner with the dunce hat on."

It was apparent Arkansas was bent on stopping the passing game.

"They were dropping nine, 10 guys into coverage," Daniel said. "It's hard to throw the football through that.... We took what they gave us in this game. I even said, 'Coach, let's just keep feeding Tony the ball. What a courageous effort by this guy coming into his last game, because it's been a hard year for him [being injured]."

Daniel passed for 136 yards (a season low) and threw only 29 times, completing 12 (a season low). Temple was gobbling up real estate at a record rate. He broke Rice's Dicky Moegle's mark of 265 yards rushing set in the 1954 Cotton Bowl against Alabama. Going into the Cotton Bowl game, the 5'9", 205-pound Temple had 758 yards rushing and eight touchdowns on the season after suffering an ankle injury against Nebraska in early October and missing the rest of that game and two more contests.

With Missouri comfortably ahead in the fourth quarter, Temple was on the sideline with a "tweaked hamstring." Missouri's coaches and Temple were aware he was short of the 54-year-old Cotton Bowl rushing record

"We were deciding whether we were going to put him back in or not," Pinkel said. "Our trainer Rex Sharp came up to me and

Tony Temple (22) dances into the end zone for a touchdown against Arkansas in the third quarter of the Cotton Bowl on January 1, 2008.

said, 'I think he can go.' I went up to Tony: 'Do you think you can go?' He said, 'I will let you know.'"

Shortly thereafter, Temple said he could go. And Pinkel just told him to hang on to the ball. He did on a dazzling 40-yard touchdown run, which made him an unlikely Cotton Bowl record holder and hero instead of Arkansas's two-time Heisman Trophy runner-up Darren McFadden.

Missouri's defense used its safeties in the running game and utilized some shifts up front to confuse the Arkansas blockers and McFadden, who played his last college game. Temple played his final college game as well. Missouri and Temple game up their appeal to the NCAA to get another year for Temple, who played one game late in the 2004 season, when he carried the ball six times and suffered an ankle injury against Nebraska.

Even without Temple, Missouri is being ranked among the top five teams in the country heading into the 2008 season, with 16 other starters from the Cotton Bowl game returning. Five juniors—Moore, Coffman, Daniel, defensive tackle Ziggy Hood, and defensive end Stryker Sulak—submitted their names to the NFL advisory committee for feedback, but Missouri announced they will return for their senior seasons.

And for the senior starters who are leaving, along with the injured Pig Brown, it was a milestone season they have left behind.

"I know the history of Missouri," said MU's nose tackle Williams, a senior. "It has not had the best of luck. It has had the fifth and the kicked ball incident. When we got here, [offensive coordinator] Coach [Dave] Christensen and Coach Pinkel told us we were about the dream. Our class, when we got here, we said would be the class to turn it around. And I think we have done a great job."

sources

Broeg, Bob. Ol' Mizzou: *A Story of Missouri Football*. Huntsville, AL: Strode Publishers, 1974.

Columbia Daily Tribune, 1987–2007.

Cotton Bowl Media Guide, 2007.

The Dallas Morning News, 1987–2007.

El Paso Times, 1973.

FedEx Orange Bowl Media Guide, 2005.

Fifth Down, Football Writers Association of America newsletter, 1967–72.

The Gator Bowl Association website. http://www.gatorbowl.com/.

The Kansas City Star, 1978–2007.

Lawrence Journal-World, 2001.

McCallum, John D. *Big Eight Football*. New York: Charles Scribner's Sons, 1979.

Miami News, December 1960.

MIZZOU, 1957–2007.

Official 2006, 2007 NCAA Division I-A and I-AA Football Records Book. Indianapolis, IN: The National Collegiate Athletic Association, 2006, 2007.

Smith, Loran. *Fifty Years on the Fifty: The Orange Bowl Story*. Charlotte, NC: Fast & McMillan Publishers, 1983.

Savitar (University of Missouri yearbook), 1894–2006.

Southern Methodist University Football Media Guide, 2006.

SouthernMethodist University Sports Information Department archives.

Steele, Michael R. *Simply Devine: Memoirs of a Hall of Fame Coach*. Champaign, IL: Sports Publishing, 2000.

St. Louis Post-Dispatch, 1960–2007.

St. Louis Globe-Democrat, 1959–60.

Sugar Bowl Media Guide, 2004.

University of Michigan Media Guide, 2003.

University of Missouri Baseball Media Guide, 2006.

University of Missouri Football Media Guide, 1974.

University of Missouri Football Media Guide, 2005, 2006.

University of Missouri, Official Athletic website of the Mizzou Tigers. http://mutigers.cstv.com/.

University of Missouri Sports Information Department archives.

University of Oklahoma Football Media Guide, 2004.

University of Nebraska Football Media Guide, 2003.

University of Notre Dame Football Media Guide, 2003.

University of Texas Sports Information Department archives.

University of Texas at El Paso Football Media Guide, 2006.

about the author

Steve Richardson, a Dallas-based freelance writer, has covered college sports since the late 1970s. He worked at the *Kansas City Star* and later at the *Dallas Morning News* for more than 20 years combined. He has served as a special correspondent for college basketball for several publications. This is his seventh book. His other titles are *University of Texas Football Vault: A Story of the Texas Longhorns; A Century of Sports: The Centennial Book of the Missouri Valley Conference; Ricky Williams: Dreadlocks to Ditka; Kelvin Sampson: The OU Basketball Story*; and *Tales from the Texas Longhorns*. Richardson recently served as editor for 60 Years of the Outland Trophy. He also collaborated with Rare Air Media for ABC Sports College Football All-Time All-America Team book and worked with All-Pro Cliff Harris on the former Dallas Cowboy's second book, which was released in the fall of 2006. He has been a correspondent for *Sports Illustrated* and written freelance articles for numerous publications, including *USA Today*. Richardson, a 1975 graduate of the Missouri School of Journalism, has collected writing awards while working in three states. He has covered 24 Final Fours, all the traditional major bowl games, professional sports, and two Olympics. He was the president of the United States Basketball Writers Association in 2002–03 and has been executive director of the Football Writers Association of America since 1996. He also had internships at the *Kansas City Star* and *Cincinnati Enquirer* before graduation and worked a year at the now-defunct *Shreveport Journal* before moving to Kansas City.